Transformation in Christ

Also by Professor Devine:

Our Living Liturgy. Chicago: Claretian Publications, 1966. **Why Read the Old Testament?** Chicago: Claretian Publications, 1966. **To Be A Man** (ed.) Englewood Cliffs, N.J.: Prentice-Hall, Inc., 1969. **Theology in Revolution** (ed.) Staten Island, N.Y.: Alba House, 1970. **New Dimensions in Religious Experience** (ed.) Staten Island, N.Y.: Alba House, 1971. **That They May Live: Theological Reflections on the Quality of Life** (ed.) Staten Island, N.Y.: Alba House, 1972.

GEORGE DEVINE
Chairman, Department of Religious Studies
Seton Hall University

Transformation
In Christ

alba house alba house A DIVISION OF THE SOCIETY OF ST. PAUL
STATEN ISLAND, NEW YORK 10314

Library of Congress Cataloging in Publication Data

Devine, George, 1941-
  Transformation in Christ.

  Includes bibliographical references.
  1. Theology, Catholic. 2. Christian life
--Catholic authors. I. Title.
BX1751.2.D395   248'.48'2   70-39884
ISBN 0-8189-0240-X

Nihil Obstat:
  William H. Winters, O.F.M.Cap., S.T.L.
  Censor Librorum

Imprimatur:
  James P. Mahoney
  Vicar General, Archdiocese of New York
  February 4, 1972

  The nihil obstat and imprimatur are official declarations that
a book or pamphlet is free of doctrinal or moral error. No
implication is contained therein that those who have granted
the nihil obstat and imprimatur agree with the contents, opinions
or statements expressed.

Designed, printed and bound in the U.S.A. by the
Pauline Fathers and Brothers of the Society
of St. Paul, 2187 Victory Blvd., Staten Island, N.Y.
10314 as part of their communications apostolate.

FOR
Joanne and Byrd

Foreword

This book first began to take shape quite a few years ago, after I began teaching theology to undergraduate students at Seton Hall University. It became evident to the members of our Department that reliance on a single syllabus or text would be wholly inadequate in leading students to an understanding of the human situation and the religious implications of man's life as he discovers himself in the world. So it became especially necessary to emphasize creative teaching through a variety of approaches, all the while taking care not to sacrifice scholarship for the sake of popularity, or unity for the sake of diversity. In the intervening years, there have been many changes in the circumstances and vantage points of students and professors alike, and in theological scholarship and speculation, as well as in the various pedagogical approaches employed in religious studies. The present volume is by no means the best or only approach; it is not the same one I myself used even a few years ago, nor is it certain that it is what I would follow a few years from now. But it does represent, somewhat, a distillate of what I, and some of my colleagues both at Seton Hall and on other campuses, feel to be popular treatment of Catholic faith, practice and problems in a context which is honestly contemporary, but which tries to exercise a necessary reliance on tradition. One of the changes that is evident today is the reduction in the number of courses or semester hours in which a student is concerned with theology or religious studies, in the new curricula of so many of our colleges. This book will attempt, without necessarily becoming *"the* text" (something I've tried to avoid in the past), a readable exposition of some key concepts in Catholic theology as a point of departure for further student contemplation and reading and for dialogue with other students and with professors.

Also, it is to be hoped that, while my main concern has been with college undergraduates, the subjects discussed herein may be of some interest to the general Catholic readership in an age when the Church as a community seems bewildered by dogmatic liberals and dogmatic reactionaries alike. But those who read these pages will likely be disappointed if they search for "liberalism" or "conservatism." True theological inquiry and teaching cannot be the servant of either camp, and I suppose that some will be offended by the apparent "liberalism" of some of my remarks, just as others will be turned away by the seeming "conservatism" of others. There might well be a certain pacific atmosphere in the womb of pseudo-traditionalism, and even the hubbub of extreme radicalism within the Church offers a certain sure consistency. But to embrace either pole is not to serve ourselves or the Church. As Gerard S. Sloyan observes: "We are the transition people. The transition will be painful and consume us in any case. Nothing can be done to make it smooth or easy. We are under obligation not to lose courage or to misread the signs of the times. Like a pilot who sees his aircraft imperiling the lives of children on a schoolyard, we must think of others more than ourselves. Since we are about to lose our lives, we might as well follow the gospel injunction and save them by doing it voluntarily."[1]

New York City, March 17, 1972   George Devine

1. Gerard S. Sloyan, "Planning for the Future," **Liturgy** 16:5 (May, 1971), p. 5.

Acknowledgments

The author is indebted to all of those who have encouraged this work since its beginnings, and this includes a host of students, colleagues and friends whose names by themselves could occupy a volume. Special thanks are in order for several fine friends and colleagues at Seton Hall University, particularly Rev. James M. Cafone, Prof. Joan T. Nourse, and Prof. Donald H. Wimmer who gave the author much encouragement. The most helpful single individual was Prof. Gerald Pire, of the Department of Religious Studies, who afforded the author advice and inspiration throughout the preparation of the text. Also especially helpful in their assistance at various stages of the book's gestation were Rev. Msgr. Alexander F. Sokolich, Rev. C. J. McNaspy, S.J., Mr. Michael Gubernat, Rev. Andrew M. Greeley, Mrs. Ruth Dolan, Miss Laura Waage, and Mrs. Margaret Chiang. The author is also thankful for the encouragement of Mrs. Anthony Gran, Dr. Philip Scharper, Rev. Edward J. O'Toole, Mr. Clyde V. Kuemmerle and Dr. Helen B. Warrin.

Table of Contents

Transformation in Christ

The Honeymoon Is Over

During the early and mid-1960s, there came upon the scene
a great theological revival which put to rest the image of
religious studies as an esoteric discipline that held little to
interest the common man. While human history, since the
false security that had prevailed in America and Western
Europe just after World War II, had gone on under the
Sword of Damocles, the early 1960s began to show a glimmer of hope. The nuclear superpowers had gone to the brink
of confrontation over the missile sites in Cuba, and the up-
shot of it all was not Armageddon, but a nuclear *detente*
that some had even begun to call the *Pax Americana*. In the
domestic sphere, it appeared that injustice and bigotry between the races was gasping its last, and new programs of
social action were in the forefront at home and abroad,
especially in the dynamic new vision of the Peace Corps and
the Alliance for Progress. And, in a new and heady mixture
of the secular and the religious (much like that present in
the Semitic experience), man began to see the Spirit of God
brooding over the waters of earthly chaos, about to bring
to humanity a new order of love and peace. As Martin Marty
wrote in *America,* "Utopia was not wholly implausible. Pope
John and President John, Saint Nikita and Reverend King
would help take care of things; only mopping-up operations
for the kingdom of God were ahead."[1]

And so it was that the statesmen of the world took their

place beside the men of the cloth as the saints of the day:
Good Pope John, the earthy peasant who, supposedly a care-
taker Pontiff, heralded the greatest internal renewal in the
Roman Catholic Church in centuries, against the backdrop
of a general ecumenical movement that had been gaining
momentum for over half a century; Young President Kennedy, a personal incarnation of all that was new, bold, fresh,
visionary, honest, kind and full of that inimitable *vigah;*
The Reverend Doctor Martin Luther King, Jr., who was making non-violence an important word in the modern American
vocabulary, as he led crusade after crusade, suffered and
passed test after test, to advance the cause of equality for all
men, regardless of their race, in a new age of opportunity and
freedom. Even Nikita Sergeivich Khrushchev, strongman of
the Soviet, seemed to take on an unconventional sanctity
as he defused the Russo-American time bomb during the
Cuban crisis, and seemed to resign himself and his nation to
a *modus vivendi* with capitalism. Indeed, some even re-
marked that his style was almost like that of another pudgy
proletarian, Angelo Guiseppe Roncalli, who succeeded in
persuading Khrushchev's atheist son-in-law, *Izvestia* editor
Aleksei Adzhubei, to accept his Papal blessing.

The time was coming. It was just around the corner. They
would all get along in peace and love and harmony. Catholic and Protestant and Jew. Russian and American and
Frenchman and German. Communist and capitalist and so-
cialist. Young and old. Black and white and brown. Easterner
and westerner. North American and South American. Rich
and poor. All members of the one Family of Man, united—
whether they identified it or not—by the saving love and
grace of Jesus the Christ, moving towards the final stage of
Salvation-History. For those *cognoscenti* who had read the
notorious avant-garde Jesuit, Pierre Teilhard de Chardin,
the meaning was clear: this was the threshold of that final

unity of all matter and spirit known as the Omega Point, as proclaimed by the paeleontologist-philosopher-theologian who himself embodied one of the greatest convergences—a unity between science and the humanities, specifically religion, which seemingly dismissed all the previously apparent conflicts between the two approaches to truth.[2]

The mood of those days, however recent, may be difficult to appreciate vicariously. Those of us who remember, especially those of us who were in our twenties or late teens then, are not likely to ever forget the spirit that prevailed in the early 1960s. As a case in point, allow me to recall one brisk, invigorating autumn evening when I was a graduate student in theology at Marquette University. I had become associated with a Chicago-based group that was promoting the cause of the vernacular in the Roman Mass, a subject then under discussion at the Second Vatican Council.[3] We had recorded our *Demonstration English Mass* and sent it to all the English-speaking Bishops in the world, so our practical illustration of a vernacular liturgy might help turn the tide in Council deliberations. And we had occasion to present live demonstrations of our proposed sung Mass in English for interested gatherings of Catholics and others throughout the Eastern United States. Since I was also on the Marquette faculty then, teaching a course on liturgy, I included one of these demonstrations as a special event in the program, and we drew about seven hundred to Brooks Memorial Union that night. The atmosphere was charged with imminent renewal in the barnacle-encrusted Holy Mother Church we had come to love, but also to be impatient with. While the crowd seemed awed by the chanting of the Mass prayers (including the Canon) in their native tongue, the dignity of the reformed ritual, and so forth, perhaps the mood of the demonstration Mass was best symbolized by the intentions chanted in the Prayer of the Faithful: "For our Holy Father, and all our Bishops . . . ;" "For the success of the Council . . . ;" "For the passage of just and effective civil rights legislation . . . ;" "For President Kennedy and all our public officials. . . ."

My roommate, a fellow theology student who had taken part in the liturgical demonstration, joined in the unwinding afterwards, over a few containers of Milwaukee's favorite beverage, and began to express the enthusiasm so many of us felt then: "I mean, everything we've studied about the sacred in history, and God working through time and space, the whole convergence bit of Teilhard, I can really see it in our times now! Everything with Kennedy, and the civil rights movement, and how the countries are starting to get along, it all makes so much sense! We're really entering a new age, a new spirit, like we've been studying and talking about in class. Boy, this is a great time to be alive, to be part of it all. . . ."[4]

And that, my friends, was the evening of November 21, 1963.

It is hardly necessary to recall what happened to our President and to so many of our dreams and ourselves the next day in Dallas. But young people—or people in a youthful mood—have a certain resilience, and it was entirely possible to regard the tragedy of that Friday afternoon as an isolated blemish on the log of our great voyage. Since then, of course, we know what has happened: even though man has taken a step onto the moon's surface, and the Mets have won the World Series, we have seen the repetition of election-by-assassination in this seemingly civilized society of ours, the outbreak of violence in the streets of most major cities in America, the conversion of national nominating convention into bloody brawl, and the gap widening between young and old, black and white and brown, rich and poor, man and man.

When violence and discord became the trademark of the late 1960s, the vocabulary was no longer one of convergence and non-violence, but of *power:* who has it, what to do with it, how it should be distributed. And this in the context of revolution, usually in the violent sense—if not implying physical brutality, then at least inferring the dramatic rending asunder of individual identities and social institutions as we have known them.[5]

And those who saw a religious significance in the history of the early sixties have not failed to see a religious significance, of an opposite sort, in the events of the days since then. As Sal St. John Buttaci says in his poem *Requiem for the Good*, it is a feeling like that experienced by the child who sees his dog buried and asks, for the first time, "Where is God?"[6]

Too many of the old certainties seem gone forever. The God who always took Our Side in war. The neat, safe world we had come to expect, all ready to move into. And the sort of neo-renaissance spirit of "all this, and heaven too!" that seemed to glimmer in the early years of the last decade. Gone.

For some, the answer seemed to be the "Age of Aquarius," probably not as wide-eyed and certainly not as naive as the optimism of a few years prior, and perhaps heavily laced with mock seriousness . . . often a disgusted, alienated dropping-out, if not turning-on.[7]

And one must wonder about the results of too much reliance on flower-power. It is already on the wane, from all external appearances, and those who hang onto the observable ritual are likely to be the few who jumped onto the bandwagon after it collapsed and was deserted. This is especially apparent when one considers that the utterances of *om*, despite the soothsayers of the 1967 march, failed to make the Pentagon turn orange and levitate as promised, that Claude, the hero of *Hair,* winds up going into the Army, and that most young revolutionaries have had a tendency to sow their last wild oats before that all-too-soon day when they must purchase monthly commutation tickets for the 8:17 out of Hoboken.[8]

But, despite the obvious shortcomings of the "hippie" counter-culture,[9] it should be clear that there is no solace to be found in attempting to turn back to a world that is, in many ways, no longer there to go home to. If the 1960s have been called the "decade of disillusionment,"[10] the 1970s are the decade of future shock and culture shock, a time when man realizes that his world is changing at such a dizzying pace that he really doesn't know quite who he is any more.[11]

We are just now, I think, beginning to realize the impact of occupational identity crisis upon the individual person in the world. Despite the fact that we continually insist that vocational roles are accidental to the worth of the person, we are now face to face with a new world in which individuals who have competently prepared for a role in society will, in a large percentage of cases, be unable to fulfill the role envisioned or one akin to it. A case in point, of course, would be education, where the glut of available personnel is expected to endure through 1990,[12] thus dashing to bits the Horatio Alger legend for a generation of Americans in at least this one major dimension of human activity. And yet, those who wind up losers in the numbers game have already passed a certain point of no return psychologically: they have been prepared for certain professional aspirations since they were children, through years of schooling, and have often made direct preparation for such emotionally-invested societal roles as will now be denied to them—through no real fault of their own—for at least the bulk of their employable lives. This situation became very real to me when, in the Fall of 1970, one of my freshman classes at Seton Hall University was composed largely of education majors who were relatively certain that they wouldn't find positions upon graduation, but who were already enrolled in college and needed to take advantage of a breather in *academe* before plotting a next move.

I use the example of the educational profession not only because I am close to it, but also because, as experts have made clear, it is one of those vocational roles which will be in jeopardy, for the foreseeable future, regardless of any recovery in the American economy.[13] Even if we see a coming-to-fruition of the many optimistic predictions of the American government, the white-collar slump, caused by an overproduction of liberal-arts educated personnel for some decades, will remain with us. Since many of those who read this book will be, to greater or lesser extent, liberal-arts educated people, the crisis should be a familiar one: that feeling of being all dressed up with no place to go.

The same sort of crisis has made its mark on the aerospace technician, the construction worker and numerous others during the recent negative atmosphere in the economy. And we are beginning to see that we have too many people prepared for too few jobs to be performed. There are various possible solutions to this problem. One is genocide of a sort: massive doses of euthanasia, abortion and the like.[14] Another is to ignore the problems, to simply allow the rich to get richer and the poor to get poorer, thus hastening the world's rushing pell-mell towards a holocaust wherein the haves fight it out with the have-nots. The *tertium quid* would be to begin attempting a new way of looking at persons in society, so as to stop identifying them so closely in terms of their vocational functions.

This, indeed, may be the wave of the future, and it is likely to manifest itself in a variety of changes in our way

of life: further development in the direction of a welfare
state wherein, even in a competitive capitalistic context,
many individuals are sustained by the society not because
of what they can produce, but simply because of who they
are . . . or more simply, *because* they are.[15] Also, there is the
trend towards compression of the individual's working years
during his lifetime. In many categories of public service
(police forces, fire departments, transit workers and the like)
there is increasing realization of the fact that men who are
much over forty years of age should be allowed the option
of retiring at a substantial pension and allowing younger,
more vigorous men to take their turn at the strenuous duties
involved in the work. This means, though, that the society
must compensate the individual for as many as sixty years,
in exchange for about twenty years of direct services. This is
possible only when the society as a whole alters its prevail-
ing attitudes towards work *vis-a-vis* the right to be, and
tangible productivity as justification for the individual's
existence in the society here and now.

But in any case, it is apparent that man's understanding
of himself in terms of societal function is no longer the stable
verity it has seemed to be for so long. Gone are the days
when a son could confidently prepare to step into his father's
profession, secure in the knowledge that he would never
leave his home town (except perhaps for a jaunt at an ivy-
covered college) and would marry the nice girl next door,
delighting in the role he would play in his community until
he became too old or too rich to work at it. But also gone,
apparently, is the new type of adventure which has characterized so many of our younger people, who envisioned
their entry into many of life's new horizons. If the lawyer
son of a lawyer is coming upon hard days, so is the broad-
caster son of a butcher, who realizes that the upward mo-
bility of his society, with all its   ational opportunities,

cannot cure the supply-and-demand problems of an economy whose job market has become first of all top-heavy, and probably glutted in general.

Recently I came to know a young history instructor who seemed to embody, in so many ways, the problems of which I am now speaking. He had gone to the magnificent public colleges of his native California, and migrated to the East Coast to do some college teaching while finishing his doctoral dissertation. By the time he was about to become a full-fledged Ph.D., he was finding himself virtually unemployable. Not only had the academic market collapsed under him, but the escape routes he had counted on were rapidly closing as well. A roundly-educated man, he often amazed me with the breadth of his brilliance. Bearded and carrying about a flowered bookbag, he plodded across the campus in bright red tennis shoes, seeming to symbolize all there was about the young intellectuals that was coolly revolutionary. But he had to pay the rent. And by the time he was putting the finishing touches on his variegated and impressive preparation for service to the world, he was having serious difficulty, literally, paying that rent.

My friend, usually able to maintain a sort of good humor about things, began to philosophize about the predicament which was affecting him and so many others. Speaking from the vantage point of his historical expertise, he opined that the only way for an individual to survive in the world of the latter part of the twentieth century was to be as flexible as possible in occupational capacities, to meet the changing needs of an unpredictable economy. Further, he submitted that the average individual might well find himself making his way in the world in as many as half a dozen disparate societal functions during his working lifetime.

Thus, there seems little stable identity in envisioning oneself in the role of professor or bus driver or ecologist or politician or journalist or iron worker. And this in the socio-economic system which appears to be the world's healthiest. We are literally living in the age when one must do a lot of very fast broken-field running simply to keep apace. This necessarily occasions each person—most especially each young person—to constantly ask, "Who am I? What is my identity? Where am I going?"

Almost a decade ago, when I began teaching theology to undergraduates at Seton Hall, our glances at the "human condition" seemed to resemble a sort of tourism. We necessarily spoke in terms of teeming masses in India who were ill-clothed and unfed, of hard-core unemployed in the ghetto of Newark, of human cogs in the impersonal machinery of totalitarian Marxist regimes, or of the "freaks" in our own environment who had, somehow inexplicably, opted for drugs or booze as alternatives to reality, or the "hollow men" who refused to "get involved" as Kitty Genovese was murdered in Queens.

Today it is different. Those who used to think of themselves as God's Elect (whether or not in terms of the Puritan or Jansenist ethics that have so deeply influenced Christian thought in our culture) now realize that there is no guarantee on one's place in this world or the next simply because of being white, or American, or twentieth-century, or educated, or a respectable, Church-every-Sunday citizen who was so much better than "them." Today we are realizing the truth of John Donne's words, "No man is an island," and coming to a gut-understanding of human interdependency.

We understand, largely due to the recent economic downturn (as it was euphemistically termed by the White House), that the fates of Wall Street seriously affect the sales of theater tickets on Broadway, and that the layoffs at Grumman on Long Island substantially influence the chances of a secretary's finding work in Manhattan. These and numerous other factors have helped us to realize that our self-concepts, based on societal functions, are largely dependent on the stability of other people's self-concepts, based on the security of their own societal functions. The viability of (for instance) Vincent Sardi, Jr., as restaurateur is genuinely dependent on the viability of David Rockefeller as banker, and that if both of those roles seem to be impersonal, they are in fact determinants of who those individuals will be in society, where and how they will live and function, even—ultimately—whether they will have to line up at the welfare office or the soup kitchen. (I would be surprised to see these gentlemen there, but it *is* possible!)

But the domino effect goes much further, of course. We know, too, that the questions of war in Southeastern Asia or the Mediterranean, famine in India or China, political instability in Moscow and Peking, economic uncertainty in San Francisco and Seattle, elections in New York and Pennsylvania, all may be very much interrelated. We know that whether or not we are headed for a violent revolution in the West will be, to an ever-increasing degree, influenced by what does or does not happen in the East.

If I were to illustrate the change I am describing by a simple example, it might be this one: during the many urban riots in the long, hot summer of 1967, President Johnson had called for a national day of prayer.[16] True to form, the TV broadcasters covered day-of-prayer activities around the United States, and one of the locations they selected was Washington, D.C., a city which offers a most graphic example of urban squalor and bitter ghetto frustrations. In the Washington excerpt on the TV newscast, the viewers were taken to the well-kept, beautifully landscaped campus of one girl's college in the Northeast district of the city, where a bevy of nuns in impeccably laundered and starched habits walked around the tranquil campus, chanting Psalms in a variety of musical settings that would tickle the palate of any liturgical-music gourmet (I seem to recall the works of Somerville, Gelineau and Deiss). This was the sisters' prayer. And I have no doubt that it was as sincere as any. But I was so disturbed by the implication that the "trouble" in Washington was something "out there" somewhere. By the inference that good nuns were praying for all the poor people "there" and not for themselves as being among the people who were in one way or another all the poorer for what was happening in Washington. I am in no position to judge whether this unsavory connotation came from the sisters or from the TV network. And I am sure it was entirely unconscious on the part of all concerned. Indeed, some of this meaning was undoubtedly supplied in the eyes of the beholders. And that is precisely to the point. For I am submitting that, nowadays, we simply would not look at the phenomenon of trouble in the ghetto, or hostility in Northern Ireland, or famine in Asia, in the same far-off way that we would have just a few years ago. The "human condition" is no longer seen as external. No longer something through which the student might be escorted by the professor with gun and camera.

No. Now it is here. It is not out there. It is you and it is me. It is we who fear for our livelihoods in the world of culture shock and future shock. It is we who fear for our lives in war, foreign or home-grown. It is we who live in a culture where injustice and selfishness and dishonesty and hopelessness seem to be increasing all around us, and where the friendly neighborhood pusher, even in the "best" residential areas, offers ready escape to all who can pay, from the grade-school level on up.

It is we who live in a society marred by student riots and political assassinations, and the grim reminders of urban blight and bloody conflict in the streets. It is we who live in an age when the best hopes of men have succumbed to some of their worst fears.

Unlike the more innocent days of yesteryear, we no longer need view "the human condition" through spectacles that have been artificially tinted. Or by way of a special course of study that smacks of "slumming." Or vicariously, through a selection of graphic and dramatic films or novels.[17] All we now seem to need is a mirror.

And many of the theological nostrums that carried us through before will no longer soothe us if we are disturbed by the reflections we perceive. It will not help, any more, to take comfort in mechanically-dispatched gestures of peace, or to be forever singing "Alleluia" hymns to the tune of the tambourines where we feel that we can hardly breathe under the weight of our own crosses, or to say that we see God's plan working itself out through secular history.

That would have kept us quite happy—even thrilled us— in those euphoric days only a decade ago. But now the honeymoon is over.

1. Martin Marty, "A Warning to Catholic Extremists," **America,** 119:5 (August 31, 1968), p. 123.

2. Teilhard's attempt to explain human progress in evolutionary terms is expressed comprehensively in his **The Phenomenon of Man,** tr. Norman Denny (Evanston, Ill.: Harper and Row, 1959).

3. Our organization was the Friends of the English Liturgy. The unlikely name comes from the "friends" who put up the money for our record and book publishing ventures. The group later became known as F.E.L. Church Publications, and moved to new headquarters in Los Angeles. F.E.L.'s best-known contribution to the liturgical music scene to date, is not the **Demonstration English Mass,** ironically, but the liturgical folk music of Ray Repp. While the **Demonstration English Mass** drew laudatory comment from many Bishops and liturgists, and many of the liturgical revisions embodied suggestions from it, the actual F.E.L. proposals, and the identity of F.E.L., became lost in the "shuffle" of liturgical renovation in 1964-65.

4. The quotation is, of course, a paraphrase. The Marquette roommate was Randolph F. Lumpp, now a member of the religious studies faculty at Dayton University. Prof. Lumpp agrees that the paraphrase is substantially accurate.

5. Cf. my introductory essay, "The Age of Aquarius," George Devine, ed., **Theology in Revolution** (Staten Island, N.Y.: Alba House, 1970).

6. Sal St. John Buttaci, **Requiem for the Good, The Bayley Review,** Spring, 1965.

7. Devine, **ibid.**

8. **Loc. cit.**

9. Cf. Myron B. Bloy, Jr., "The Counter-Culture and Academic Reform," in George Devine, ed., **New Dimensions in Religious Experience** (Staten Island, N.Y.: Alba House, 1971), pp. 257ff.

10. John Cogley, among others, has used this phrase.

11. Cf. Alvin Toffler, **Future Shock** (New York: Random House, 1970).

12. Fred M. Hechinger, writing in **The New York Times** (January 3, 1971), has done one of the best analyses I have read of this subject.

13. The day after Hechinger's article, mentioned in the previous note, was published, the President held a televised conversation with news correspondents, in which Nixon again expressed the optimism of his Administration concerning the American economy. While Nixon and his advisors may be somewhat expert and even correct concerning the fates of the stock market and the GNP, the type of economic-occupational chaos of which I speak would be upon us regardless of anything right or wrong done by a federal Administration of any party. And a news story in **The New York Times** (March 7, 1971) indicates that the economic-occupational imbalance of which I speak is spreading in England.

14. Many good treatments of this topic are now available; one of the best, in my opinion, is James V. Schall, **Human Dignity and Human Numbers** (Staten Island, N.Y.: Alba House, 1971). Also cf. the essays in George Devine, ed., **That They May Live: Theological Reflections on the Quality of Life** (Staten Island, N. Y.: Alba House, 1972).

15. In some situations, I think, we have already reached the extreme of sustaining individuals **because** they are, to the point where there is something of a profession in the propagation of an increasing number of welfare recipients. Unless serious and substantial reforms of welfare laws and procedures become effective soon, it will continue to be the case that the law will favor the welfare recipient over the unskilled laborer and the illegitimate child over the poor child whose parents are married and share the same roof. I am not arguing here that welfare monies should suddenly be withdrawn from all recipients, but simply suggesting—as has President Nixon—that we cannot continue to administer welfare equitably under existing laws, routines and criteria, without fostering the notion that overpopulation among the poor is a sort of marginally profitable way of rebelling against and weakening the Establishment. Accusations of "white middle-

class morality" notwithstanding, the poor themselves would benefit most from a welfare system which favored the ghetto worker over the non-worker, and which seriously discouraged people from conceiving children if they were not prepared to support them in the context of some sort of familial structure, with all the parental responsibilities typically involved therein. While the squalor of ghetto life helps one to understand the meaning of **proletariat**—those who have only their children—perhaps it is counter-productive to continue supporting the notion that a child, whether or not properly cared for in a familial situation, is always better than none at all. A change in this situation will mean a very real transformation of attitudes and psychological orientations among many, and I believe that would be fostered by a welfare system which placed more emphasis on incentive, with the understanding that the welfare system would take up the slack, when individual effort based on incentive simply didn't take care of all the needs.

16. That day, I had gone to a simple prayer service at my parents' parish in San Francisco, where I was spending the summer. The pastor, at the morning Masses, had invited all the parishioners (and anyone else who cared to come) to a brief praying of the Rosary that Sunday afternoon. About fifty people came to pray the Rosary, and we left after about fifteen minutes' time, with a final blessing from Monsignor Cahill. But the significant thing is that the congregation, reflecting the demography of Holy Cross Parish, was about half black and about half white. Somehow, this prayer service for racial harmony seemed more meaningful to me than all those I was to see on TV later that day.

17. This sounds odd, perhaps, coming from a professor who offers a course called "Religious Dimensions of Media Experience." But it is precisely the type of thinking I express in these pages that causes me to approach media experiences quite differently from the way I did a few years back. It seemed to be the fashion, then (unfortunately), to fit works of literature or cinematic art, or what-you-will, into already-furnished theological cubbyholes. Now, I favor a study wherein media expressions are respected, in all their integrity, for their own sake, and studied in a fashion which is truly interdisciplinary. Only then can the study be really profitable. Future courses of this type, I believe, will be offered by professors whose academic competency is as strong in some field(s) involving media (literature, film, drama) as in religious studies, for students who are as likely to be majors in English or communications arts as in religion or philosophy.

Who Will Rescue Me from This Body Doomed to Death?

In the previous chapter, I maintained that desperate man was too ready to grasp the early 1960s as a jewel woven into the fabric of Salvation-History, and that this has led to much disillusionment, over the past few years, that has been as much religious disenchantment as secular. Perhaps our religious leaders are just now beginning to realize some of the implications of this. In a book I edited in 1970 called *Theology in Revolution,* Andrew M. Greeley touched on the subject in a most interesting way, suggesting that in the liturgical renovations of Vatican Council II, the Church managed to adapt itself to the secular spirit of the times as man was about to get sick and tired of the secular spirit of the times.[1] In his own inimitable style, the famous author submits for our consideration something he self-effacingly calls "Greeley's Law . . . As soon as everybody else starts it, Catholics stop it."[2] Greeley was referring, in this context, to the penchant for the mystical that seemed to characterize the "hippie" youths who were staying away in droves from the streamlined American religious experiences of their former churches: ". . . the hippies and the Merry Pranksters are putting on vestments and we're taking them off; we have stopped saying the Rosary and they're wearing beads . . . we are making our new low-church liturgy as symbol-free as possible and they are creating their own liturgy which is filled with romantic poetry and symbolism."[3]

It would be entirely too glib to demean the serious and scholarly preparation for liturgical reform which went on in the Catholic Church prior to the actual changes effected by Vatican II,[4] or to suggest, even half-jokingly, that the liturgical restorations were occasioned by anything less than the weight of sound theological understanding and a healthy respect for authentic Catholic tradition. But a most grotesque coincidence did indeed take place in the mid-1960s, so far as the Catholic experience of liturgy is concerned. Just as congregations around the world were beginning to benefit from a liturgical renewal that should have taken place well before the Middle Ages, just as liturgical experts like C. J. McNaspy were beginning to hail a Mass where the mystery remained, but not the mystification,[5] the scene was being set for man's disenchantment with a new sort of religious experience which seemed characterized by familiarity and fluidity, and appeared to be a celebration of the secular as the masterpiece of the Divine genius.

When man's euphoria over his here-and-now began to degenerate into an anguished cry of O tempora! O mores!— when the honeymoon was indeed about to end—a religious identity crisis was a necessary concomitant. To a large extent, this is due to the over-reaction that took place in the post-conciliar changes in the liturgical experience. Catholics (especially the Irish) were schooled in an awe of the sacred, to the extent that they subconsciously considered it at least venially sinful to talk in Church or to call a priest by anything but Father (even if the priest were one's own son).[6] They now became a bit giddy with the novelty of some real theological and liturgical needs like congregationally-participated Betsingmesse[7] or a versus populum altar. Our associations with the Mass had been so dour for so long that perhaps it was natural to begin singing a host of mediocre plinkety-plunk guitar hymns that bubbled over with love and joy and peace to the point of saccharine monotony.[8] We had for so long neglected the centrality of *Alleluia!* in our faith that it was probably understandable that the pendulum should swing in the direction of neglecting the mystery of the saving Passion and Cross of Christ.[9]

And the upswing was tremendous in its impact, especially upon the young, for a while . . . but only for a while. Let us not be so naïve as to suppose that all of the disaffection of youth with the institutional Church can be reduced to matters of poor liturgizing. But I submit that a case can be made for the viewpoint that a sudden response to a new "upbeat" in the liturgy was bound to peak and then break in any case, and when the "upbeat" was riding on the crest of secular history, then it was all the more precarious.

If all of this is understood, then the observations of Greeley, cited earlier in this chapter, make profound sense. This is especially so when one realizes the peculiarities of the *American* Catholic experience. The far-reaching reforms of Vatican II have surely had their effect in Uganda and VietNam and Belgium, but not in quite the same way as they have in New York and Oakland and Joliet, where reform in the Roman Catholic Church—especially visible, accidental, external reform—put an end to many of the labels that distinguished a suspect immigrant minority from the American mainstream. Catholics no longer had to order separate meatless dishes at Friday business luncheons, were no longer subject to the old gibes about "hocus pocus" and "Benny's got all the dominoes," were no longer called "mackerel-snappers." What is more, a Catholic President who became an international martyr-hero showed the falsity of all the caricatures about tunnels from the White House to the Vatican or governmental suppression of Protestants and Jews.

For once, American Catholics were being *liked.* They were able to partake of that important American delicacy known as being one of the gang. The ghetto walls were crumbling, and it was no longer necessary for diocesan newspapers and Catholic magazines to keep writing about how Loretta Young was a Catholic, or how the Governor of such-and-such State was a Catholic, or how Notre Dame would defend the Faith against the infidels on the gridiron Saturday.[10]

Catholics in America had made it, were part of the American fabric. And, while this assimilation was enhanced by seemingly secular events, the causes were seen as being chiefly religious ones, and this was a positive quality in the American Catholic experience of the 1960s. But it later came to pass that Americans of all religious groups began to question the American Dream.[11] For American Catholics, this would necessarily mean questioning the reformed Church that had helped them become senior partners in that Dream.

The new woes—international and domestic—that became woven into the fabric of the American experience in the latter 1960s and the beginning of the 1970s seemed to occasion a sudden wave of nostalgia among all those who were just old enough to greet the world around them with anything but the bravado of youth. While America in general sought solace in romanticizing the "happy days" of the 1930s and 1940s,[12] or paying dearly for standing-room admission to the Broadway revival of the 1925 musical *No, No Nanette,* starring Ruby Keeler,[13] Catholic Americans seemed to suffer from their own longings for the past. But there is, of course, a major difference: even the most romantic and nostalgic Americans knew that, as a matter of course, Shirley Temple would grow up, Mickey Rooney would cease playing Andy Hardy, times would have to change, and reruns of old movies on the TV late shows would be nothing more than a sentimental escape, having perhaps some therapeutic value for those who had to face a newer, bolder, more challenging world. Catholics, though, had been led to believe that the *weltanschauung* instilled in them would never admit of change. As I observed in my 1969 book *To Be A Man,* they have ". . . largely been products of a catechetical system which sincerely attempted to communicate wholly the faith life of Christ's Church, but which often seems to have made the mistake of articulating the accidental just (or almost) as forcefully as the substantial—Latin in the Mass and no meat on Friday with the Blessed Trinity and the Virgin Birth."[14]

The nostalgia of the secular order has been unable to take itself totally seriously; its participants know that they are, to a large extent, chasing rainbows. But among Catholics, the phenomenon is quite different: those who long for the religious experience of yesteryear feel betrayed at having been led into a new world and a new time which is far less secure than what they had known, and they insist that things would have held together better had the Church not forsaken the binding forces of ecclesiastical rigidity and uniformity, even—or especially—in externals.[15] The world would not be falling apart so desperately, they would insist, had the Church not allowed the well-polished jewel of the Tridentine Mass in the Latin Rite to degenerate into a Tower of Babel, and the reverential awe of the Eucharistic Sacrifice to give way to the announcement of Form B or Response II during the Canon.[16] Our children would not be tempted by heretical teachings and theological confusions, we are so often told, had we the sense to retain the Baltimore Catechism (revised edition, number two) as *the* religion textbook for all Catholic students.[17] There would be no problem about religious vocations if nuns were made to continue dressing like real nuns, and so it goes.

Before we scoff at some of these impassioned cries, let us

remember that the majority of Catholics (especially those born before 1950) had to react to externals because they had so little choice about the matter; we can hardly fault their viewpoint as superficial without somehow indicting their religious education (which we might well do, in many cases). Let us further consider the fact that, while these people have had something precious taken away from them, something which, if truth be told, is far more profound than a concern with superficial appearances—nothing has come to supplant what has been lost. To a large extent, the much-promised renewal of liturgical piety, religious vocation (in the broadest sense, mind!), effective social involvement, and other *desiderata,* have *not* come to fruition, after almost a decade of tub-thumping and dizzying experimentation. The experience, in some ways, is not unlike that of the Israelites wandering in the desert after escaping Egypt. They felt that their previous servitude under Pharaoh might have been no bargain, but it was vastly superior to the misery of the desert, and they were painfully aware of the fact that, having left Egypt, they could never return. Thus it was that they cursed the Moses who led them, and whose Promised Land had yet to materialize.[18]

To these people, the Church has offered little in the way of sympathy or companionship. They have tried, in many cases, to exercise their typical obedience to ecclesiastical authority, even when they failed to understand or agree with the programs involved. In their usually sincere, somewhat fumbling, Holy-Name-Society-Daughters-of-Isabella ways, they have attempted to adjust to *aggiornamento* in the Church they had come to know as steadfastly immutable. As reward for their efforts, they have tended to receive rebukes from liturgists for their insufficient vocal participation in the ritual, from theologians for their inherent distrust of complex speculation, from suburban liberals for their al-

leged racism. The only friends most of these people seem
to have found are in the pages of *The Wanderer* and *Twin
Circle*, or at the meetings of *Una Voce*, The Roman Forum
and similar organizations dedicated to preserving the Catholic milieu of the past, or, more often, restoring it once it
has been taken away. If the Catholic community has offered these people much in the way of company, it has been
in the form of the theological demythologizers who, in too
many cases, have succeeded in swiftly and brutally destroy-
ing religious faith in practically everything except their own
slick jargon. And the religious publishing trade, having lost
much of its business from the people who used to thrive on
safe, *Imprimatur*-bearing Catholic devotional books, has
often felt it necessary to compete with Hollywood in its
promotional campaigns, and thus tends to advertise a new
book and/or author in terms of its quarry: this one, friends,
will blast to bits the Our Father and Hail Mary; the next,
the physical resurrection of Jesus. Another will take on the
Eucharistic Presence of Christ. The next will reconsider the
morality of bestiality. Is it any wonder that the religious
book business is alienating the conservative and boring the
radical?[19] I hardly intend to suggest that serious theological
speculation is worthless or frivolous, but only that it is bound
to suffer when its publishers insist on marketing it with the
same techniques used to sell *Portnoy's Complaint* or *Everything You Always Wanted to Know About Sex but Were
Afraid to Ask.*

But if the disappearance of the solid, never-changing
Church has been a jolt to the oldsters, hasn't it been a boon
to the coming younger generations? In all honesty, I don't
really think so. This is no criticism of reform in the Church;
indeed, I am still scorned as "too liberal" by more Catholics
than I care to enumerate. But the Church, having changed
in the *way* that it has—suddenly, without adequate prepara-

tion or instruction (despite the warnings of the Popes and the Vatican Council about this), pell-mell, helter-skelter, crazy-quilt—has managed not to shore up its own resources for a new and meaningful encounter with the world, but simply to render itself somewhat incredible as an institution having authority. It is still on record as the Church that doesn't change, but seems preoccupied with siezing every opportunity to do away with jots and tittles, whether the case in point be mixed-marriage canons, St. Philomena, Sunday-observance-on-Sunday, women in the sanctuary, St. Christopher, particular or general absolution, host-in-hand communion, Eucharistic Prayers II, III and IV and Penitential Rites A, B and C.

In a way, perhaps, the Church is going through something like the housewife who has allowed cobwebs to accumulate for so long that, when she finally gets down to cleaning the place, the effort is necessarily haphazard: whole clumps of dust remain untended while a cherished vase is struck down by the errant mop-handle; a stain on the rug cannot be removed easily, so a chair is moved to cover it; a chronically crooked mirror refuses to be straightened at all, and is taken down to the basement to be punished and think about its ways for a while; the incessant whining of the vacuum cleaner disturbs the neighbors terribly, but the machine is so clogged that it achieves no purpose; a rickety old end-table is finally and angrily thrown into the garbage can after years of limping and insufficient service; the furniture is all dusted and polished to a mirrorlike gloss; the dining room table is set with impeccable taste but there remains no time to get the shopping done; a new and expensive piece of *bric-a-brac* is displayed prominently in the living room . . . and all because Mother-in-Law is coming to visit.

Mother-in-Law, in this case, would be the World Outside the Church (that place where Leonard Feeney had said there would be no salvation),[20] and it appears cruel indeed to suggest that perhaps Mother-in-Law is not so concerned with the efficacy of the house-cleaning job as our imaginary *hausfrau* might believe . . . but perhaps we are beginning to feel that it is true. Especially when the Church's intramural public-relations job has been so awkward (or, often, simply absent) as to leave its membership befuddled rather than liberated or educated for a new age.

And how can youth view such an institution? Probably in the same light as other authority structures—the family, the school, the government—in which it has tended to lose faith of late. For many of our young people (they tell me), the Church seems to have no more credibility than the parent who drinks martinis (even moderately) and condemns marijuana, the policeman who ignores an anti-strike injunction (even justifiably) and continues to insist on strict law enforcement, or the peace candidate who (even unavoidably) leads the nation even further into an unpopular war.

In this regard, even a generation which seems prepared for a Consciousness III world of flux will be hard put to live with the inconsistency of authority structures, the Church included.[21] Indeed, elders may more readily understand or adjust to an authority structure which has to change its procedures owing to unforeseen factors, even to comprehend the emergencies which might occasion reneging on a promise, although insisting rightly that promises should not be made if it is at all doubtful that they can be honored. But young people, whatever they may proclaim, seem more dependent on consistency than anyone else, even the very old. They are perhaps the most intolerant of all generations when it comes to hypocrisy, real or alleged, disorganization, or failure to embody Kierkegaard's notion that "purity of heart is to will one thing."[22]

As the prominent psychologist, Eugene C. Kennedy, has insisted, young people need authority structures against which they can polish the rough edges of their own developing egos.[23] This does not mean that every parent must be an inflexible ogre, the sort about which practically everyone's first novel is written.[24] Nor does it mean that a stern regimen in the home, by itself, is any guarantee of a loving or healthy familial relationship. It does mean, though, that a youth cannot even rebel effectively or meaningfully if he has no idea of what he is rebelling against or reacting to, if the authority figures in his experience are amorphous.

It would be absurd, of course, to suggest that the Church should have forestalled all reform, all internal renewal, for the sake of providing stability for any of its constituents, young or old. However, the case can be made that the necessary reform of the Church could and should have taken place in a manner which was more opportune for manifesting the abiding consistency of the identity of the Church as a body which admits of organic growth and development, much along the lines described by Cardinal Newman in his famous *Essay on the Development of Christian Doctrine.*[25] This would have meant, too, that some of the reformers should have exercised more prudent economy in determining their priorities for changes, e.g., the de-Latinization of the Church was an urgent need; the de-Philomenizing of it probably was not so pressing a problem, and could have been deferred until the dust had cleared from more important alterations. Another example of this, surely, would be the silly hubbub which developed over whether or not women were required to wear head coverings when attending church, when other, far more important matters were being let go, or being obfuscated by such trivia as the hat-or-not issue.

In any case, the Catholic experience of the past ten or so

years, at least in America, has at best been most unsettling
for practically all concerned. It has left us a Church which,
even if nominally intact, is badly splintered. At one extreme
of the ecclesial continuum, we have those who are psychoemotionally, as well as intellectually, prepared to resist the
least suggestion of change. To these, the slightest accidental
change signals the advent of further change, and that would
be disastrous. Their point of view, logically, leads them to
an attempt to be at least a little more Catholic than the
Pope, and in order to reconcile their position with the necessity of obedience to the Supreme Pontiff, they intimate that
the Holy Father is all right himself, but that he is subject
to a variety of diabolical influences that besiege the Barque
of Peter daily, and that even the infallible successor to
Cephas may be misled by them in non-essential matters.[26]
At the other extreme, of course, are those who intuit that
every alteration, however trivial, is the harbinger of whole-
sale renovation, and that herein lies the only hope for the
Church of the future . . . or the future of the Church. To
such persons, the infallibility given the Church, proclaimed
by Vatican Council I,[27] clearly resides in priests who excori-
ate their Ordinaries for institutional racism, or in theologians
who dissect and reject a magisterial utterance; just as clearly,
the Pope simply doesn't mean it if he implies that Mass cannot be celebrated validly (not to say licitly) by a hippie in
a telephone booth who improvises the words of institution
from the writings of Kahlil Gibran over a box of Cracker
Jack and a Dixie Cup full of Fresca.

These two groups, of course, are amazingly similar in
their relentless dogmatism, their refusal to trust anyone's
viewpoint but their own. They will tend to kneel adoringly
at the feet of a demagogue who tells them just what they
crave to hear, then quickly reject him if his own individual
thinking or conscience should happen to stray from the party

line. At all events, though these different extremists are all too obvious, they are by no means predominant within the Catholic community. For, if there be such a species today as the typical Catholic, we can say that regardless of age, sex, walk of life, geography, education or whatever, this is a sincere but extremely confused and beleagured person, bewildered and annoyed by the angry voices that shriek at him from the extremes, badly shaken by the loss of a Church which he could both love and become impatient with, but in any case discern and understand.

There is a real kind of death here, the dying of an era, an experience, a sub-culture, almost (though not quite) a Church. And this at a time when there seems to be a kind of dying all round us: the death of a whole kind of world that seemed so much more stable and comprehensible, so much more manageable and inhabitable. We had come to believe in the *Pax Americana*, even in a delicate balance, and now can be much less sure of that. We had come to know and agree with the words of the famous *Desiderata* said to be found at Old Saint Paul's Church in Baltimore (1692): "Keep interested in your own career, however humble; it is a real possession in the changing fortunes of time,"[28] and have now come to know a new world in which there will be precious little occupational stability. We had come to believe that God created the universe for the prudent use of mankind, and have come to the sickening realization that man has so abused his environment as to make our air unhealthy, and our heretofore healthful fruit and fish and other foods hazardous for consumption.[29]

Indeed, the famous Scriptural admonition that "he who seeks his life will lose it"[30] seems embodied in many facets of our current ecological crisis. A generation that believed smoking to be innocuous—what with medical endorsement of various brands of cigarettes,[31] has been upbraided by the

Surgeon General's reports on Smoking and Health,[32] and the news that over a hundred thousand doctors have quit cigarettes. Those who were led to believe that the hazards of overweight could be fought with diet soda were startled by the revelation that their cyclamated beverages were so probably carcinogenic as to warrant their speedy withdrawal from the grocery shelves. Those who were told that diets high in saturated fats could cause heart disease were encouraged to eat plenty of tuna and swordfish, then learned that these often contained dangerous amounts of mercury.[33] It is as if there is no use: the man who seeks to prevent his demise will often find that he is unwittingly hastening it.

Despite any confidence man might have had in himself and his world, he now tends to mirror the despair of Sartre and Camus, to believe that life is an ongoing absurdity, terminating only in death, the ultimate existential absurdity.[34] Seeking the wisdom of the ancients, he may ask the questions posed by Job,[35] only to arrive at the same "answers" posed by that piece of Old Testament sapiential literature: that man should not question his almighty Creator, and that the good and faithful man is rewarded after all, upon acknowledging his dependency on his God. And neither "answer" emerges as genuinely satisfactory. Man is still plagued by life, and life plagued by death.

So much has been said and written to make us less uncomfortable about death, whether in the poetry of romantics or the eschatology of theologians. Yet the dominant theme remains one of horror. The deaths of Housman's "athlete dying young" and Shakespeare's *Romeo and Juliet* seem tinged with a glow of beauteous meaning, but ultimately wasteful, and the blissful image of St. Joseph going to God in the arms of Jesus and Mary is much less familiar to us than the newsreels of Jack and Bobby being gunned down in Dallas and Los Angeles, Dr. King being picked off by an assassin in Memphis, or the kid from down the block having his head blown off—maybe even by mistake—somewhere in Indochina.

Our radical fear of death is so profound that we attempt, as if whistling in the dark, to discount it as a serious probability within the foreseeable futures of our own personal histories. We speak often of "*if* I die"; seldom of "*when* I die." Death is something that happens to the other fellow. Somehow, we continue to believe that we can avoid death if we are careful enough, that dying is but a punishment for too much high living or recklessness, for failure to take good care of ourselves. And while it is true enough that a variety of stupidities can hasten death, or a host of sensible precautions defer it, each of us will die sooner or later. Yet we dare not admit it, in our heart of hearts. To do so would be to accept our contingency, to acknowledge that the world that functioned before our birth can do so after our death, that even the most important and famous among us are dispensable.

The universal inescapability of death comes home to us, in a way, when the veterans of life whom we always thought would live forever, having survived many a crisis, finally succumb, as in the cases (recently) of such giants as Churchill, Eisenhower and de Gaulle. But, of course, the point is made far more dramatically when we see someone who is not yet old collapse in the midst of performing his duties. The deaths of Adlai Stevenson and Gamal Abdel Nasser, not long ago, are cases in point. Less famous, of course, would be the story of a fourteen-year-old boy in New Jersey who was walking to church, and dropped dead so instantly that his nose and glasses were broken when his face fell to the sidewalk, or of a high school basketball star in California who had passed all the medical examinations imposed on athletes, and dropped dead on the court in the middle of a rou-

tine league game. We are so often told by our churchmen
that death is not the end of everything, but only the beginning. Not a separation from the world we have known, but
even a deeper involvement in the universe and its meaning.[36]
And yet our dominant image of death remains that of a
violent interruption of our plans, a catastrophic cutting-short
of our lives.

Even the death of the elderly seldom conforms to the
ideal of a "happy death"[37] that has so often been preached
to us. There seems little to rhapsodize about in the picture
of death which takes place gradually, as the last chapter in
a saga of senility, loneliness, pain, confinement, immobility
and the inability to control one's bladder and bowels. If
Housman's athlete dying young is spared certain visions that
may be happy, he is spared certain visions that are sure to
be unhappy. Those who die at an advanced age are not
spared them. They may experience the isolation of being one
of the last—indeed, *the* last—of their contemporaries to leave
this world, the futility of being unwelcome guests in a world
that has passed them by, the uneasiness of being a burden
to a bevy of anxious heirs and heiresses who grumble about
the costs of medical care for their failing ancestor, fearing
that a "long goodbye" may leave less money for them to
inherit.

In the classic Christian view of the human condition, life
is indeed a series of sufferings shot through with death, and
this precisely because of man's basic alienation from himself,
his fellow man and his Creator. In the pivotal passage of
Romans 5, Paul declares that ". . . sin entered the world
through one man, and through sin death."[38] The implications
of this passage have been debated—for their own sake and
in the total context of Romans—at great length by exegetes.
What are we to derive by way of insight from this Biblical
witness? First, it is obvious that the translation is crucial.

The translation I have chosen to cite here is that of the Jerusalem Bible,[39] not only because of its fine reputation among Scriptural scholars and theologians, but also because (a posteriori), its treatment of the passage in question appears to me the most consonant with the bulk of the theological evidence concerning its meaning. The Jerusalem Bible commentary explains Romans 5:12 by noting that "Sin divides man from God. This separation is 'death,' death spiritual and eternal; physical death is the symbol of it."[40]

If we look at Romans 5:12-19 all together, it is obvious that Paul means to contrast "Adam" with "the new Adam," Jesus. The first brings death; the second brings life. Adam takes man away from God; Jesus brings him back. This explanation of things might have gone unquestioned in Paul's time, and for centuries thereafter. But how explain Romans 5:12-19 in light of the probability that hominization—the becoming-human stage of evolution—took place not in terms of an "Adam and Eve," but in the context of several pairs of first parents? This question is still being debated by theologians, as it is by biologists. We shall not undertake an exhaustive study of the question here and now, but let us note the following: (1) the probability of such hominization by way of what theologians call polygenism (more properly termed monophylism by biologists) does not constitute a fact, nor is it likely to do so, in such a way as to necessitate its being a basis for any theological explanation; (2) the reluctance of the Church to accept any biological explanation of man's origins which would threaten revealed dogma has been expressed in such a way as to direct theologians toward cautious speculation, but not to stifle such.[41]

In any event, the doctrine of original sin, as expressed by Paul in the first century of Christian history, and as wrestled with by theologians in the twentieth, clearly states that man is separated or alienated from God, his Creator, who is the ultimate source of all life, light and love, and that this rupture—effected somehow by man's rejection of the divine initiative of love—is so basic, so truly at the root of man's existence in the world, that it can best be described as original, as endemic to the very origins of humanity.

This concept may be difficult for us to grasp if we think of "sin" only in terms of an isolated historical action concretely performed, e.g., "Last night at 9:42 I committed a mortal sin, then at 11:13 a venial sin; today at 7:20 A.M. another venial sin," etc. While we have no cause to deny the reality of actual sin, we must think more basically in terms of sin as a basic alienation of man from the One who called him into being and sustains him, and who alone contains the meaning of life. It is in this context that we can understand the notion of sin as manifesting itself not only psychically or emotionally, but indeed physically. It is now that the simple language of the Genesis narrative of the Fall takes on a more profound meaning than we might have suspected: when man rejects the very word of life, from the very source of life Himself, he will experience the pain of this separation in myriad facets: spiritually, to be sure; intellectually, yes; psychoemotionally, of course; but even physically. Even in the way man lives. Even in the way he dies.

The Jesuit theologian R.J. Pendergast has dealt with the relationship between original sin and the physical dimension of humanity most interestingly.[42] Pendergast wishes to eschew any suggestion of the anti-physical bias that for so long colored Catholic theology (e.g., the implications of original sin being transmitted by intercourse since this is a concupiscent and thus imperfect way of propagating humanity, etc.). Yet he insists that original sin can and moreover does manifest itself in all dimensions of man's life-experience, the physical definitely included, so that man's very bodiliness is somehow affected by his basic alienation from God.

Rahner takes up the same notion when he speaks of death. According to Rahner, had man's history not been adversely oriented at the outset by original sin, by man's basic and radical rejection of God's invitation into friendship, there still would have been an end to life, but it would have been the sort of smooth transition Rahner has described in his treatise *On the Theology of Death,* an active, free, personal self-realization wherein the individual spirit becomes more integrally immersed in the world and the spiritual and physical realities within it, not the sort of violent, unwelcome and often sudden gear-grinding kind of demise we tend to think of. The elements of interruption, horror, uncertainty, isolation are not a part of death *per se,* for Rahner. They are only part of man's experience of death as affected, as thrown off, by virtue of original sin, by man's somehow, at the beginning of his history in the world, receiving but rebuffing God's offer of divine love and friendship.[43] The lines of communication between man and God are now defective, though still operative, and this in all dimensions: spiritual, intellectual, emotional, psychological, and also physical.

Thus, it is why we are afraid. Why we can deceive and be deceived. Why we have Excedrin headaches. Why we have neuroses and dyspepsia. It is why St. Paul himself can lament, "I cannot understand my own behavior. I fail to carry out the things I want to do, and I find myself doing the very things I hate."[44] It is the same lack of human wholeness—integrity, the theologians have preferred to call it—that causes J. D. Salinger's famous character Holden Caulfield, almost two thousand years later, to complain, "I keep making up these . . . rules for myself, and then I break them right away."[45] Theologians describe man's lack of integrity as being so pervasive that man cannot direct himself wholly towards any object, be it good or evil.[46] To put it more crudely, man is so at odds within himself that he can't even be perfectly evil.

In a way that strikes at the very root of human history, man has rejected the opportunity to belong to God in a relationship of friendship. And this initial (or original) rejection so alienates man from his Creator that he must be reunited to Him. It is not a case of mere bad example or unhealthy environment, to be overcome even by heroic effort, as Pelagius might have it,[47] but a case of a real separation between the human and the divine, a genuine breach to be healed. It manifests itself in a series of little "dyings," a continuum of experiences in which man finds himself less than truly alive. Our existential awareness of our situation is replete with symptoms: war, hatred, injustice, tragedy, loneliness, sickness and pain. This is not to suggest that there are no moments of natural happiness in life; there are indeed many. But they can never obliterate the presence (real or potential) of the awful dimensions of human life we have just described. Our life is thus less than a real life. It is shot through with death. The fact that we may not be lonely, may not be painfully ill, may not be dropping dead, this moment, does not mean that we cannot be, or that we will not soon be. In any event, we are all dying. All making our way to the grave, at varying degrees of speed. And every time we are rebuffed by another, or feel remorse at our own having been less than human towards a fellow man, or know the anxiety of trying to make our way in this perplexing world, we die a little.

With all of our heart-transplant operations and civil-defense warning systems, cancer-care units, anti-coagulant drugs and auto-safety campaigns, we don't have a really steady grip on life, any more than the ground above the San Andreas Fault is really *terra firma*. And each day—psycho-

logically, intellectually, emotionally, spiritually, physically—
we learn a little more of what it is to die.

If we are to be honest, we must utter the words of Paul:
"What a wretched man I am! Who will rescue me from this
body doomed to death?"[48]

1. Andrew M. Greeley, "Dynamic Theology—Today and Tomorrow,"
in George Devine, ed., **Theology in Revolution** (Staten Island, N.Y.: Alba
House, 1970), pp. 26-27.

2. Loc. cit.

3. Loc. cit.

4. For a digest of the theological and historical development of the
liturgical renewals of Vatican II, see my brief treatment **Our Living Liturgy**
(Chicago: Claretian Publications, 1966). The bibliography at the end may
be helpful for the reader who desires more thorough detail.

5. C. J. McNaspy, **America** 109:6 (August 10, 1963).

6. I actually knew a priest whose own father insisted on calling his
son Father on all occasions. The situation is perhaps amazing, but by no
means incredible, and may help to point out how well Catholics, especially
the Irish, have been trained in awe of anything religious. (Being of Irish
descent myself, I can make such a remark.)

7. This is one of the many German words that translates as a phrase,
"pray-and-sing Mass," which probably describes the post-Conciliar liturgy
better than outmoded categories like "high," "low," "sung" or "recited"
Mass. Interestingly enough, **Betsingmesse**, with vernacular hymns, was part
of the German liturgical tradition long before the reforms ushered in by
Vatican II.

8. Do not misunderstand: that I am a staunch advocate of **good** liturgical folk music is a matter of public record. However, I maintain that,
when much music in one idiom is being produced by many people during
a short period of time, the bulk of it is apt to be mediocre or worse. Cf. my
regular columns on liturgical music which were published in **The Advocate**
(Newark, N. J.), **Topic** magazine section, 1967-70. Also cf. my review of a
"Rock 'n' Roll Mass," **Worship** 41:4 (April, 1967), pp. 249-250.

9. For a good explanation of how the centrality of the Resurrection was
ignored among Western Catholics for centuries, cf. Godfrey Diekmann's
brilliant address to the North American Liturgical Week in 1962, just as the
resurgence of theological work on the Resurrection's soteriological role was
becoming popular. **Thy Kingdom Come** (Seattle, Washington: The Liturgical
Conference, 1962).

10. I literally remember watching a big Notre Dame-Oklahoma game on TV one Saturday, and hearing one of the Notre Dame players, interviewed after the Irish victory, telling the sportscaster and the audience, "We won this game for the Catholics in the State of Oklahoma!"

11. It is currently the thesis that the classic American dream of open opportunity is in serious trouble because of the population-education-economy crunch I referred to in Chapter 1, and that a serious rethinking of the American dream is in order if we are to survive as a nation. In this light, note the interesting suggestion of Garry Wills that Richard Nixon is in reality the last of the great American liberals. Cf. Garry Wills, **Nixon Agonistes** (Boston: Houghton Mifflin, 1970).

12. During the summer of 1970, CBS-TV presented a weekly program of music and other entertainment in the style of the 1930s and 1940s; it was entitled "Happy Days."

13. **No, No, Nanette,** presented as it was in 1971, was not overacted or "camp," but essentially played straight, and won out-of-town raves before its Broadway opening—and subsequent success—at the 46th Street Theatre on January 19, 1971.

14. George Devine, "Changes," in **To Be A Man** (Englewood Cliffs, N.J.: Prentice-Hall, Inc., 1969), p. 6.

15. In this connection cf. **The Critic** 29:3 (January-February, 1971). The whole number is a cleverly-done "Catholic nostalgia" issue. Perhaps the best piece is "A Farewell (Quite Fond) to the Catholic Liberal" by Garry Wills, pp. 14-22.

16. One prominent Catholic intellectual who feels strongly along these lines is the eminent philosopher Dietrich von Hildebrand, whom I heard give an impassioned lecture on the decadence of the liturgy at Fordham University in New York on December 11, 1970. Cf. Dietrich von Hildebrand, **Trojan Horse in the City of God** (Chicago: Franciscan Herald Press, 1967). While I respect von Hildebrand and his many achievements and contributions, and sympathize with some of his arguments, I feel that he has given short shrift to numerous very important historical facts involved in the renewal of the Roman Rite during the Second Vatican Council and shortly thereafter. However, he does articulate the position of many serious individuals who take issue with the current state of the liturgy in the Western Church.

17. After my appointment by Archbishop Thomas A. Boland to the Religious Education Advisory Council for the Archdiocese of Newark, N.J., I was amazed to see the vehemence with which so many Catholic parents insisted that their parish schools and CCD programs utilize the Baltimore Cathechism and teach religion "just as it was taught to us," in opposition to many of the new catechetical series and approaches available, which had survived the scrutiny of our Council, and which in some cases were quite excellent.

18. Cf. Exodus 16:3. All biblical citations unless otherwise specified are from **The Jerusalem Bible**, copyright © 1966 by Darton, Longmanns & Todd, Ltd. and Co., Inc. Used by permission of the publisher.

19. Cf. the remarks of myself and others on this subject in "13 Authors' Forecasts on the Crisis in Catholic Publishing," **The National Catholic Reporter**, April 17, 1970.

20. Feeney, a Jesuit priest in the Archdiocese of Boston, took the expression "Outside the Church there is no salvation" so literally as to consider all non-Catholics damned. Ironically, he was refuted by the Holy Office at Rome, which insisted that salvation is possible for all men of good will. Cf. **AER**, CXXVII (October, 1952), 307-11.

21. Cf. Charles Reich, **The Greening of America** (New York: Random House, 1970), for an exposition of a new spirit among youth which he describes as Consciousness III.

22. This is, of course, the title of Kierkegaard's famous work.

23. Father Kennedy has written much along these lines. My reference, specifically, is to a lecture I heard him give at Manhattan College in New York in 1969.

24. Scholars of literature are in essential agreement that an author's first novel is usually a **bildungsroman** ("growing-up novel") taken from the author's own struggles in achieving manhood or womanhood, often involving conflict with one or both parents. Indeed, the commonplace use of a German term indicates that the phenomenon is by no means limited to English literature. Examples of the **bildungsroman** abound in popular novels, e.g., James Joyce's **A Portrait of the Artist as a Young Man**, D. H. Lawrence's **Sons and Lovers**, etc.

25. London: Longmans, Green & Co., 1897.

26. In the lecture I referred to previously, Dietrich von Hildebrand asserted that the **Ordo Missae** promulgated by Pope Paul VI in 1970 was the work of a "Mafia" in the Church, and applied the same epithet to such bodies as the International Commission on English in the Liturgy (ICEL). Cf. fn. 16, **supra**.

27. DS 3073; cf. the article on the Vatican I treatment of infallibility by John P. Doyle in George Devine, ed., **New Dimensions in Religious Experience** (Staten Island, N.Y.: Alba House, 1971), and Hans Küng's **Infallibility? An Inquiry** (Garden City, N. Y.: Doubleday, 1971).

28. For some time, there has been some dispute concerning the original source of the **Desiderata** text; cf. **The New York Times Book Review**, query section, February 28, 1971.

29. Cf. the essays on the quality of life in George Devine, ed., **That They May Live: Theological Reflections on the Quality of Life** (Staten Island, N. Y.: Alba House, 1972).

30. Matthew 16:25; cf. Luke 14:27, 17:33, John 12:25-26.

31. Many of us can well remember the numerous physicians who, in

the years after World War II, allowed their names and pictures (in medical uniforms) to be utilized in endorsing cigarettes for their safety—especially Camels because of the beneficial effects of the "T-zone" (it stood for "throat," I recall). Presumably, this was beneficial for the pocketbooks of the physicians, who themselves had no reason to suspect that cigarettes were harmful. It would be another decade before serious doubt would be raised in the medical profession as to the harmlessness of cigarettes.

32. The initial report, linking cigarette smoking and lung cancer, as well as with tendencies towards other maladies (e.g., heart disease, emphysema, etc.) was published in 1964. There have, of course, been other reports and studies since then.

33. In February of 1971, reports were circulated to the effect that tuna then available on the American market was not as dangerous as had been feared, but that much swordfish was, and would have to be withdrawn immediately.

34. For an understanding of the existential philosophers, there is, of course, no substitute for a comprehensive bibliography of their own works. For the beginning student unable to pursue a concentrated study, but interested in the major themes of twentieth-century existentialist philosophers, especially as pertaining to religious questions and meanings, I would recommend Anthony T. Padovano, **The Estranged God** (New York: Sheed & Ward, 1966), especially the earlier portions of the book.

35. The story of Job, representing the wisdom of Judaic thought, is dated as early as the fifth century B.C. by such scholars as Myles M. Bourke, but when William Foxwell Albright, the distinguished Biblical archaeologist, visited our theology faculty at Seton Hall in 1965, he mentioned that his studies were persuading him in the direction of dating Job in the second or even first century B.C. In either event, the relevance of the Book of Job to modern man's life-experience is demonstrated by the success of Archibald McLeish's adaptation in the form of a modern verse play, J. B. (Boston: Houghton Mifflin, 1958).

36. Cf. Karl Rahner (tr. Charles H. Henkey), **On the Theology of Death** (**Quaestiones Disputatae**, No. 2. New York: Herder & Herder, 1965), Chs. 1 and 2. This is the second translation into English. The first, by W. J. O'Hara, was published, also by Herder & Herder, in 1963. Henkey's translation is generally regarded as somewhat more critical, though it does contain some problems. It is generally the more available now, too. In 1965, at the New York region meeting of the College Theology Society (then called the Society of Catholic College Teachers of Sacred Doctrine), at Marymount College in Tarrytown, N. Y., I participated in a discussion with Henkey and several of my colleagues in the Society concerning his recent translation of Rahner's **Zur Theologie des Todes**, and it was evident that not all the difficulties had been solved.

37. Some churches have instituted societies—whose membership is usu-

ally of elderly people—who pray and prepare for the ideal of a happy death. The Jesuits at St. Ignatius Church, in San Francisco, had the Confraternity of the **Bona Mors**; in Milwaukee, at the Church of the Gesu, the same order had the Happy Death Society (a vernacular equivalent).

38. Romans 5:12.

39. Garden City, N.Y.: Doubleday, 1966. The number of scholars who collaborated on the Jerusalem Bible is impressive not merely in quantity, but in terms of the reputations of the individuals. Alexander Jones was the general editor.

40. **Ibid.**, p. 275, fn. "i."

41. The ecclesiastical **caveat** on polygenism was expressed in Pius XII's 1950 encyclical letter **Humani generis** (cf. DS 3897). While Pius wanted to prevent polygenism from becoming the standard pulpit or classroom explanation of human origins, since he failed to see its compatibility with the dogma of original sin as illustrated in Romans 5 (thus his ". . . cum **nequaquam appareat huiusmodi** . . .") it is not implied that he meant to frustrate speculation on the question by theologians in the private forum of their discipline. In any case, it is clear that what is now needed is some breakthrough in theological expression which can accommodate a polygenistic stage of hominization. It is equally clear, to me at least, that such is yet to be achieved, in that the attempts made so far, e.g., those of Jean deFraine, Robert T. Francoeur, et al., do not explain original sin without falling into the difficult positions of Pelagius and/or Erasmus.

42. Cf. R. J. Pendergast, "The Supernatural Existential—Human Generation and Original Sin," **Downside Review**, January, 1964, pp. 1ff.

43. Rahner, **op. cit.**, pp. 34f.

44. Romans 7:15. Again, the translation is that of the Jerusalem Bible.

45. J. D. Salinger, **The Catcher in the Rye** (New York: Bantam Books, 1964), p. 63. I am quoting from the paperback edition that is popular today: **The Catcher in the Rye** was originally published in New York by Little, Brown and Co. in 1951, after portions of it were published in **Collier's** (December, 1945) and **The New Yorker** (December, 1946).

46. Cf. Pendergast, **art. cit.**

47. DS 225-230; 238-248.

48. Romans 7:24. Again, from the Jerusalem Bible.

—**❈[3]❈**—

If Christ Is Not Risen, Our Faith Is in Vain

Not long ago, I was giving a lecture in an adult-education series at a parish in New Jersey, and the subject came round to St. Paul's references to death, specifically in the Epistle to the Romans. During the question and discussion period, one lady asked me, "Do your students at the university really come to grips with death, with the fact that they're going to die?" I felt I was not merely joking when I replied, "They don't even believe they're going to turn thirty, let alone die!"[1]

On my way home that evening, it occurred to me that perhaps much of the tendency that youth has to celebrate itself is a way of dealing with death, *via remotionis:* a way of affirming oneself in the face of eventual doom, so as to stave off the ultimate demise.[2] Young people seem to be running away from any realization of death. Yet, in another way, perhaps they have been extremely close to it: it has been their own generation, after all, that has died in Indochina and at Kent State—while other generations have frantically sought renewed youth with wigs, corsets (male and female), toupees, face-liftings and a variety of other means that might make even Ponce de Leon wonder.

When people assess the role of religion in their lives, I believe that the key factor, acknowledged or not, will be the

way in which religion deals with death. A while back, CBS-
TV presented a "special" on the Catholic Church. I was ex-
pecting one of the usually trite and superficial treatments of
the Church in an age of crisis, the obligatory scenes of nuns
playing guitars in Des Moines, the dome of St. Peter's, and
all the other elements of the "relevant" portrayal of the "tensions gripping the centuries-old Church in these turbulent
times." In this program, there was still a certain element of
that. But the pleasant surprise was the fine narration by
Luigi Barzini. In the beginning, the program presented several scenes of funeral services, with Barzini's remark that this
was the ultimate concern of Catholics.[3] A bit dramatic? Yes,
but tastefully done. And the point was made.

Today there is much talk about whether or not religion
(in general, or a particular religion) is relevant. To be
relevant, we are told, religion must hit us where we live.
True enough. But it is at least as true that religion, if it is
genuinely relevant, also hits us where we die. If life ines-
capably leads to death, it is not enough for religion to make
sense of life, but it must ultimately make sense of death. In
fact, it must really make sense of death first, before it can
make sense of any other dimension of life as we experience
or attempt to understand it.

So it was that, in his television presentation, Barzini
zeroed in on the Catholic faith as making sense of death.
His implication was that, whatever the activities throughout life of those who were even peripherally members of the
Church, their ultimate concern remained with death.

Over the centuries, while Jesus has been revered for his
life and person, or remembered for his teachings, while
scholars and theologians have investigated and debated an
array of questions pertaining to his divinity and humanity,
the central fact about Jesus is that he meets death head on.
Jesus is centrally important to man because Jesus deals with

the very matters of life and death themselves.

Traditional expressions of theology have reminded us that Jesus died as a result of and in satisfaction for our sins. Karl Rahner, while not denying the traditional teaching, asks us to look at it in a slightly different way. In his study *On the Theology of Death*,[4] Rahner emphasizes that death, as we know it, is the ultimate symbol of alienation between man and himself, man and fellow man, man from his God. Thus it is that, if Jesus is to be truly Messiah, if he is to really deal with the human condition, he must deal ultimately with death itself. Thus the ministry of Jesus, wonderful in myriad aspects, is most worthy of emphasis for its own sake, yet finally makes sense in terms of the mystery of his death and resurrection. However, this must be understood in the proper light.

For some time, Catholic theology—or at least popular Catholic piety—seemed entirely too moribund. To forget the Cross is one thing; to dwell upon it excessively is yet another. Anyone who is presently more than twenty or so years of age can probably remember that the teaching, preaching and praying of the Catholic community (I am not speaking here of the Eastern rites[5]) seemed to focus on Good Friday as the central point of the Holy Week liturgy, if not of the entire liturgical year. *Tre Ore* was the supreme measure of Catholic loyalty for many. Unless one were sick, or for some other grave reason prevented from doing so, it was expected that he would abide with the Lord during the agony of the crucifixion, from noon until three o'clock on the afternoon of Good Friday. For numerous Catholics, it became a veritable endurance contest. Pastors were often hard pressed to fill all of the three hours' time. The official liturgy of Good Friday, centering in the Mass of the Presanctified,[6] even combined with the Stations of the Cross, and veneration of the Cross, simply did not last long enough.

Often, there was recourse to Christ's Seven Last Words, in some form or another—sometimes in sermon, sometimes in musical rendition by a choir (e.g., Dubois' version), sometimes even both. Yet, often enough, it was not quite three o'clock—and sometimes it was well in advance of the hour —when the churches found that they had nothing more to occupy their congregations for the afternoon. No matter, though, to the steadfast, who kept watch with the Lord until the ninth hour of the day, recalling the biblical narration of the Passion.

The emphasis here, for the most part, was upon the suffering we had inflicted upon Jesus by our own sins, however trivial we may have considered them to be. It was common for a preacher to remind us that the most incidental misdeeds on our part were in effect little thorns woven into Jesus' torturous crown, or that even the most minute venial sin caused the hammer to strike once more at the nail that pierced one of Jesus' hands. There can be no doubt that it is ironic, selfish, and in the truest sense of the word sacrilegious for man to turn his back—even very slightly—upon the One who is all love. To reject the divine initiative of love involves a tragedy which not even the most dramatic Good Friday sermon could adequately describe. This is especially so when we consider the fact that we do this so often—sometimes unconsciously (and even a sin minus subjective personal guilt is, in the objective order, a sinful action),[7] sometimes in the name of a rationalized motive of seemingly unimpeachable virtue, sometimes out of a callous attitude which is uncaring about priorities other than our own. But what I am saying here (and the more prominent theologians and liturgists of the past two decades have said it before me) is that the type of Good Friday sermon alluded to above really tended to miss the point. The point is not that Jesus endured death because of our sins, so that had our sins been of a lesser nature or quantity, he would not have died, would not have suffered so excruciatingly. The point is that Jesus, by virtue of the very nature of his role as Savior, had to address himself to the central dimension of the human condition in the concrete order. Jesus had to encounter death. No matter what man did or did not do, Jesus had to take death in hand. For him not to have done so, for whatever reason one could imagine, would be to deal with matters incompletely, or to skirt the central issue.

What Jesus actually did in dealing with death was to contradict or override a series of human refusals of the divine initiative of love. For Jesus to do this in a way that would be at all meaningful or efficacious, it was of course required that he be truly human himself. Much of the traditional teaching about the death of Jesus as "satisfaction" for man's sins emphasizes the necessity of an equal party offering satisfaction to the offended party, viz., God offering satisfaction to God. While it is surely fitting that an offense to the Deity be rectified by a person who is himself divine, it is no less important that Jesus be truly, fully a man. The Epistle to the Hebrews stresses this: the second person of the Trinity, in becoming man, is like us in all ways but sin, i.e., he has not himself committed sin, though he enters into, takes flesh in, a human condition rife with sin and its effects.[8]

For this to make sense at all, we must discard any notion of Jesus as God "pretending" to be man, or donning the mask of humanity for the sake of a mere audio-visual device.[9] When the Prologue to the Fourth Gospel tells us that "the word became flesh,"[10] it is meant that God's "word," i.e., his communication with man, not only became human, but entered fully into everything human. We appreciate this more fully when we note that "flesh" here is originally the Greek *sarx,* denoting not merely physical substance, but everything involved in what is meant to be human.[11]

This means that Jesus necessarily entered into all manner of human situations. Interestingly enough, the Jerusalem Bible renders Hebrews 4:15 in English as ". . . we have one who has been tempted in every way that we are, though he is without sin." Clearly, if Jesus was truly a man, he was subject to all of the experiences and trials involved in human experience. This obviously means he was tempted to sin, to join in a history of human rejection of the Father, but that he did not so choose. It further means that, if his death was to make any sense or have any real effect, he must have encountered death as we do, with uncertainty, hesitation, trepidation . . . yes, fear.[12]

We may be inclined to query, "How could Jesus be afraid of death if he possessed divine knowledge all along?" If we could answer that, the hypostatic union—the true divinity and true humanity of Jesus—would cease to be a mystery. Indeed, even the more articulate pronouncements of churchmen on this subject give us no clear answer.[13] Suffice it to say that Jesus, though he be truly divine as second person of the Trinity, must be just as truly a man, a real flesh-and-blood human, and that as such, he must have experienced all of life, including death, in a way that was genuinely and profoundly human. It is here that there resides that factor of optionality that renders Jesus' human actions meaningful and ultimately salvific: the fact that Jesus was tempted but did not sin; the fact that Jesus was scared of death, as are you and I; the fact that, throughout, Jesus was not play-acting, was not enduring a charade, however painful, secure in the knowledge that God the Father waited in the wings, ready to bring rescue, vindication, glorification on cue.

Thus, Jesus in his humanity, presented with the same circumstances and options as other men, took them differently, converted the human "no" to God to a new human "yes" in response to the offer of divine friendship. When Jesus, in the

Gospel, is quoted as saying, "Father, into your hands I commit my spirit,"[14] he is voicing the sentiment which is appropriate not only to his death, but indeed to his entire life and ministry. Jesus does not die only on Calvary. He dies throughout his life. And I do not mean this in quite the same way as I previously referred to all of us dying throughout life.[15] Rather, I mean that Jesus is continually submitting himself to the divine will of the Father, through all of his life, and finally as manifested in his passion and death. This he does, not only in filial love for the Father, but in fraternal love for all of mankind. Whatever else could have motivated Jesus individually is well subjugated to his love of God the Father and of all men. It is precisely this model which Jesus will ask us to follow.[16]

Rahner expresses the meaning of Jesus' death by contrasting it with what he calls the "death of Adam." For Rahner, the "death of Adam" (which, of course, is present throughout the life of Adam) symbolizes alienation from God, indeed defiant autonomy; it is a graphic incarnation of aloneness, and is present in human death generally. But the death of Jesus is different, just as the life of Jesus is different. Jesus, in both his life and his death, incarnates not autonomy or alienation from God the Father, but rather loving trust in him, submission to his provident will, acceptance of the challenges and responsibilities involved in the divine mission. This is so throughout Jesus' life, and eminently so in his death.

So it is that Jesus' death, like his life, becomes a sign of man's responding positively, not negatively, to God the Father's divine initiative of love and friendship. Furthermore, Jesus' death becomes a prelude to his ultimate triumph over death as we have known it, in that he rises from the dead. Robert E. Neale, in his book *In Praise of Play*,[17] nominates the Lord as the supreme humorist. If this be so, then the resurrection of Jesus is the practical joke *par excellence,* in his winning out over death. The triumphant Easter hymn of the Byzantine Rite, as rendered in English, expresses it succinctly: "Christ is risen from the dead, trampling on death by death."[18] We are familiar with the old expression "fighting fire with fire," but to actually speak of trampling on death by means of death itself is to introduce an element beyond our experience and understanding. Yet Jesus does precisely that, conquers—even ridicules—death by his own death, which culminates in his resurrection. The New Testament allusions to Jesus' death make it clear that the Christian community's joy over this fact of eventual resurrection can hardly be prevented from reaching the stage of giddiness. It is as though the early Christians, in recounting the central events of their faith-life, have difficulty keeping a straight face . . . or perhaps see no need to do so.

By rising from the dead, Jesus alters the value of human death. It need no longer be the alienated or autonomous "death of Adam" of which Rahner speaks. It can be, instead, the death of the Christ, the death of the Risen Lord, a sign of a repaired relationship between God and man which manifests itself in triumph over the root symbol of the human condition, death itself as we know it. So it is that Paul will proclaim "Christ has in fact been raised from the dead, the first-fruits of all who have fallen asleep. Death came through one man and in the same way the resurrection of the dead has come through one man. Just as all men die in Adam, so all men will be brought to life in Christ."[19] And his same first pastoral letter to the Corinthians will go on to include the Scriptural cry of the winner: "Death is swallowed up in victory. Death, where is your victory? Death, where is your sting?"[20]

Numerous theologians, today, have addressed themselves to the question of whether or not Jesus actually rose from the dead in the flesh. While the more traditional or conventional theologians, either explicitly or tacitly, continue to assert belief in Jesus' physical resurrection, some contemporary scholars of religion have asserted that the actual bodily resurrection of Jesus from the dead as an historical fact is doubtful and/or unnecessary. Not the least of these is Rudolf Bultmann, who speaks of Jesus' resurrection not in terms of physical restoration to life, but rather as a continuing-to-live in the experience and faith-lives of his followers, in what Bultmann calls an "eschatological encounter" with Jesus.[21] Others have followed Bultmann in this, though he probably remains better known for his attempts at the "demythologizing" of Christian dogma.

As with most of the events of the first century, studies of history, both religious and secular, leave much to be desired, particularly with regard to the controverted events which are important to the life and teachings of Jesus. But—assuming that we are attempting to understand the teachings of Jesus' own followers and their perception of the events in question, there can be no doubting the actual resurrection in the flesh of Jesus. The preaching of the early Christian witnesses makes clear their understanding of Jesus as bodily risen just as he was bodily dead. For them, worship of a corpse would make no sense. The sacrifice of their very lives for someone who had proven a loser would be a ridiculously stupid investment. Such a sacrifice would be in order only for the sake of following one who was clearly shown as the winner, hands down, in the struggle with all the vicissitudes of the human condition, most especially death.

The one who becomes aware of Jesus' resurrection in a most striking way is Paul. Remember that Saul of Tarsus, unlike some of the others, was not a disciple of Jesus during his earthly ministry. Even after Jesus' crucifixion and resurrection, Saul—as a devoted student and teacher of the Jewish Law—sought to obliterate any threat to the proper observance of that Law and its attendant beliefs and traditions. And in Saul's time, the most obvious threat was belief in Jesus. The conversion of Saul, as narrated in the book of the Acts of the Apostles,[22] takes place precisely in the context of an encounter with Jesus who is risen and now mystically present in his members in the Church. To suppose that Saul alters the course of his life in so radical a way due to an hallucinatory meeting with a revered dead man is naïve and fantastic. And we must remember, too, the testimony of the other Apostles who did know Jesus in his earthly ministry, who did bear their own witness to his resurrection, in addition to and in ways quite different from that of Paul.

In fairness to Bultmann and other theologians or "demythologizers," we would note that there is genuine truth in any emphasis on the presence of Jesus in the hearts and lives of his followers, down through the centuries to the present day. However, if we render that presence—in the name of empiricizing or desupernaturalizing our theological expressions—a mere memorial, we commit the gross error of excising the very heart of the Christian gospel.

The Scriptures and tradition of the Church teach rightly that we are all members of, or all part of, Christ. But none of us, especially as seen in our own lifetimes, suffices for Christ. None of us can be equated to Christ. Even a very holy man is not Christ, but a part of him, of his mystical body. So it is with others, however holy or not, from the time of Paul the Apostle until today, who call themselves or who have been called "Christians." What makes us effective witnesses in the world is not that we remember Jesus, not that we have an eschatological encounter with him, not that we imitate him, not that we admire him as a wonderful man and attempt to do likewise . . . all of these are, to be sure, elements in the total reality, but the central fact is that we

are effective witnesses to Christ in the world because Christ
is in the world, through us, and he can be so, truly, only if
he is risen from the dead in the flesh, just as he died in the
flesh, so that, no longer subject to the limitations of time
and space,[23] he now relates to the whole of the world through
his members, in his body, the Church. This is precisely what
Paul saw and what he then taught.[24]

This is what singles out the followers of Jesus, what
makes them different from the followers of history's greatest
and most revered men. We may speak of Jeffersonians or
Thomists or Aristotelians or what-have-you, but not in the
same way that we speak of Christians. We may say that,
despite their deaths, Gandhi and Dr. King and the Kennedy
brothers—to mention a few—live on in the minds, hearts and
deeds of those who remain after them. But it is in no way
the same as what we say when we proclaim that Jesus Christ
is risen from the dead and dies no more, that he lives, truly
and supernaturally, in his followers, who will share in his
resurrection.[25]

We do not merely remember someone who is in fact
present. We may remember things *about* them that belong
to the past as opposed to our present knowledge of them,
but we do not merely remember them, when in fact we
experience their here-and-now presence. So it is with Christ.
We do not simply remember him, although we may well
remember certain historical facets of his activity which belong to times previous to our own; we respond to his presence as it is here and now. It is precisely by virtue of Jesus'
risen condition that he is mystically present in his Church,
in his members severally, as the dynamic risen Lord who
redeems the world.

Moreover, it is exactly the resurrection of Jesus that
renders it possible that we share in his mission, passion,
death and risen glory. In that his resurrection frees the man

Jesus (we are here discussing the Savior in his humanity) from the limitations of time and space, he becomes—as Rahner would have it—*pan-cosmic,* i.e., capable of communicating with and influencing the universe without regard to spatio-temporal limits. It is thus possible for other men to be members in him, to share in his saving activities and their benefits.[26] It is this that hits Saul on the way to Damascus, that makes him and others preachers of the Good News of the Christ.[27]

Jesus' passion/death/resurrection—considered together since these are but phases of one action, one saving event—culminates in his ascension. The Creed proclaims that Jesus sits at the right hand of the Father. This expresses, in a most apt and graphic way, the reconciliation of man to God that takes place in Jesus. The man Jesus now enjoys favor with the Father. It is true, of course, that there is no question of the relationship between the divine persons of the Trinity, as it was and will be eternally. But the intimacy that has been described in the ascension/session[28] is that between God the Father and Jesus in his humanity—Jesus in his humanity as incorporating[29] all men who will partake of the restored relationship with God that he has effected. To speak of Jesus the Word, the second person of the Trinity, as one with God the Father, is to recite a theological truism. To speak of Jesus the man as being at one with the Father is to announce the restoration of man's relationship to his creator, to the source of all life, light and love.

Jesus can be called the incarnation of the dialogue of love between God and man, the embodiment of the interplay between the human and the divine, in that he is truly human and truly divine, acting as man and as God. As God he saves man, as man he worships God. As God he makes present to man the salvific love and grace imparted by the Trinity. As man he leads in the expression of human prayerfulness and sacrifice in adoration of the Triune God.

During the last decade, some were taken aback when E. Schillebeeckx published a book under the English title *Christ the Sacrament of the Encounter with God.*[30] How is it, they asked, that we can speak of Christ as a sacrament? Is he not a person rather than a sacrament, since sacraments are obviously *things?* And, besides, we Catholics acknowledge only seven specific sacraments instituted by Christ. Actually, a sacrament (in the broadest sense) is the sensible embodiment of a situation or relationship involving persons. I mean *sensible* here not in the way that we commonly speak of things as sensible because they make sense logically, but rather in the way that they can be known through one or more of the five senses. Sacrament, in this broad connotation, does not have to mean one of the seven sacraments of the Church. It does not even mean a specifically religious thing. Simply the sensible embodiment, or the tangible incarnation, of a situation or relationship involving persons. Accordingly, a torn-down section of the central ward in Newark, never rebuilt, is a sacrament of the spirit of despair that prevails in many a hard-pressed American city; a blood-stained battlefield in VietNam is a sacrament of the awful series of relationships between the South VietNamese, North VietNamese, Viet Cong and Americans. So, too, is a Christian marriage a sacrament of the love that prevails between and through Christ and his Church in the world.[31]

So when theologians like Schillebeeckx speak of Christ as sacrament of the encounter with God the Father, they mean that he is the embodiment or personification of the relationship between God and man, a relationship of *saving worship,* in that Jesus is both *saving* (God acting as God towards man) and *worshipful* (man acting as man towards God).[32]

Similarly, if Jesus is the incarnation of our access to God, the Church is the incarnation of our access to Jesus. Or, as

Schillebeeckx put it in the same famous book, if Jesus is
the sacrament of the encounter with God, the Church is
the sacrament of Jesus.[33] This is so, of course, in the same
sense of sacrament that we just discussed, and so the Church
is the sensible embodiment of the relationship between Jesus
Christ and mankind.

St. Paul, in his first letter to the Corinthians, said the
same thing a little differently, almost two thousands years
before contemporary writers like Schillebeeckx reiterated it
for the modern world. Paul describes the Church as the
Body of Christ.[34] Those who read I Corinthians 12:4-31 will
see in this well-known passage a striking emphasis on the
interdependency of the various members of the Church and
their common dependency on the Lord. Yet to dwell on this
aspect of Paul's teaching alone would be to miss one of its
main points. For, in truth, the same idea might have been
implied otherwise, as it is in St. John's passage about Christ
as vine and the members of the Church as branches.[35] But
the main significance of the term *body* here, it would appear,
is that the Church is being stressed as the sensible, active,
effective and dynamic presence of Christ in the world. *Sensible* in that it can be known or perceived by the senses: the
Church is visible, tangible in witnessing to Christ in the
world. *Active* because its very bodiliness allows it to act concretely in a variety of situations, times and places. *Effective*
for the same reason—the Church is able to have an effect on
the world in which it acts, in which it bears witness to the
saving love of Christ. Finally, *dynamic* since it is capable of
growth through time and adaptation to a variety of needs
and circumstances.

The same idea is expressed by the Bishops of the Church,
in the dogmatic Constitution on the Church (*Lumen gentium*) from the Second Vatican Council. In the first chapter
of that constitution the Church is spoken of as a *mystery*.[36]

We commonly think of a mystery as something we cannot understand, either in the general sense or in a specifically religious or theological context (e.g., the true humanity and true divinity of Christ would be a mystery of faith, etc.). However, there are further implications to the term *mystery* in the specifically theological sense. When *mysterion* was used in the Greek of the New Testament, it meant God's plan for salvation, or a component part of it; it also meant a *sign,* whose purpose is to call attention not to itself, but rather to a deeper reality, namely a relationship between persons, in the context of a specific time-place situation.

The Church, then, is a mystery in that it exists not to call attention to itself as institution or structure, but rather to draw men to a deeper reality, namely the relationship between God and man as incarnate in the person of Jesus Christ, and as this relationship is acted out within the context of particular time-place situations and needs.

At this point it might occur to many that I have presented some fine ideas about the Church, its efficacy as embodiment of Christ in the world and as fulfilling the needs of man, which might all be very good in theory, but that I ignore those most genuine problems which today threaten the Church's effectiveness, if not its very credibility, in the contemporary world. By no means! Now into my fourth decade as a twentieth-century Catholic (especially in the perplexing circumstances of the Church in America) and into my second decade as one immersed in the study and teaching of Catholic theology as a profession, I am genuinely unable to ignore such problems, and do not believe that I would desire to ignore them were that possible. There are many things I could say about the present state and position of the Church, in general and particularly in the United States; they might well occupy another volume. But for now, let the following suffice:

First, we make a great mistake if we ignore the *dynamic* aspect of the Church, which we noted earlier. The Church by its very nature is and must be capable of growth through time and adaptation to particular needs and circumstances. Today, we see all around us myriad attempts of the Church to understand itself as a growing body, adapting to kaleidoscopic exigencies and priorities around the globe. We may wonder why the Church seems to be doing this so clumsily; we ought really to marvel at the fact that the Church is doing it at all.

Ought we to marvel because the Church is not what I said it was? Is not dynamic? Does not admit of change or development? No. But the sad fact is that, until quite recently, most members of the Church, particularly members in positions of leadership, conducted themselves as if the Church were incapable of any change or renewal. This attitude, especially evident in the late nineteenth and early twentieth centuries, came to be called triumphalism. Triumphalism embodied the conviction that the Church, like a precious jewel, had been polished to such a state of perfection that development, adaptation, renewal would be unnecessary. Triumphalists looked around at the Church as it appeared in their own timeplace situation, smiled smugly, and decreed that not one jot or tittle would ever change. Oh, perhaps the 11:15 Mass on Sunday might eventually change to 11:30, just as the pastor might eventually die and be replaced by another. But nothing else, nothing "essential," would be altered. And in the triumphalist vision, virtually everything that was observable about the Church came to be confused with everything that was essential about the Church. Triumphalists fell into the vanity of celebrating their own view of the Church as equal to authentic Catholic tradition. In a moving plea for a genuine Catholic conservatism (in the best sense of the word), Charles Kohli speaks to this problem: "I have made frequent use of the word *tradition*. I would ask you not to place that term into a column marked 'conservative' in the contemporary sense. I do not think it is fair to surrender tradition to the 'traditionalists' as they are presently defined. I am not asking you to celebrate the thirteenth as the greatest of centuries. I am not glorifying the vision of those who think that authentic Christian practice is what they knew from 1870 Rome or in 1925 Brooklyn."[37]

But in the triumphalist atmosphere (some of which remains today, as Kohli's remarks indicate) the dynamism and adaptability of the Church were ignored and even suppressed. When John Henry Cardinal Newman published his now-revered *Essay on the Development of Christian Doctrine* just before the turn of the century,[38] many intimated that he was courting heresy to suggest that Christian doctrine could in fact develop; indeed, some continued to hold that view around the time of the Second Vatican Council, where Newman's thought is said to have been influential.[39] There have been many examples of this sort of thing in the experiences of those who have labored in and for the Church in recent years.

One need only recall the prior censorship of the writings of Pierre Teilhard de Chardin, before his death in 1955. And how Greeley has publicly lamented the subtle ways in which the Jesuit scholars John Courtney Murray and Gustave Weigel were ostracized by many of their confreres,[40] who were suspicious of fellows who did too much reading, thinking and writing. There is, too, the story of the priest who was called on the carpet for preaching a sermon on the Church as the Mystical Body of Christ, a few years before Pope Pius XII articulated the same notions in his 1943 encyclical *Mystici Corporis Christi*.[41] Of course, it is easy to see how authentic tradition can become obfuscated in this sort of mess.

Given that sort of atmosphere, one can readily understand the shock waves that have rippled throughout the Church since Vatican Council II. One characteristic reaction to the conciliar decrees has been to overinterpret or overapply them, to insist that increased freedom for nuns means mandatory T-groups for all novices, that rediscovered obligations in the socio-economic order means that all priests must lead demonstrations. Another typical response is to overreact to the type of overreaction just described, to insist that the priesthood would have been just fine had it been left the way it was jointly constituted by our Lord, Bing Crosby and Barry Fitzgerald—or to sound the alarums that communion under both species is, like flouridation of water, a Communist plot.

In a word, the average Catholic became woefully oversold on the idea that everything was laid down for all eternity in simple, black-and-white terms, to such an extent that he need never anticipate change or prepare for it, and thus in matters of religion need never think, read, decide, choose. No, he need only memorize all the *minutiae* given him in the initial field manual. If today's average Catholic is not an extreme left-winger or extreme right-winger, ecclesiastically, then he is at least terribly confused, and possibly has become disgustedly apathetic. After all, if he can no longer trust and believe the changeless Church, whom can he trust and believe?

But I would suggest that the troubles of the Church today are not vastly different from those of yesterday in *degree;* they are only different in *kind.* And they are part of the dynamic character of the Church itself. Remember the Pauline image of the Church as body. A body grows and adapts while retaining its essential identity. None of us is the same as he was at age one, when it comes to height, weight, maneuverability, the power to express oneself in speech and writing, the ability to make decisions, to reason, and so forth. Yet every one of us, in matters essential to identity, is the same person. So it must be with the Church.

Yet why is the growth process so painful in the Body of Christ? We are accustomed to a certain amount of discomfort in any bodily development, such as teething, or the changing of the voice in puberty. But why the excruciating pain that attends the growth and adaptation of the ecclesial body? We can note, to be sure, the fact that the particular adaptations which seem to be required of us today are more acute than in other times, and that this might explain the intensity of the pain involved. But I would suggest that, in the current stage of the Church's life, growth has been extraordinarily painful because growth has been, in many regards, unduly retarded and suppressed.

In the Church, it seems that our growth has been retarded or suppressed in a number of areas. The liturgical problems which plagued the Roman Rite before the year 1000 were not treated even superficially until the Council of Trent which began in 1545, and not dealt with in depth until Vatican II.[42] The question of mandatory celibacy for priests in the Western Church has called for serious investigation at least since the time of Abelard in the twelfth century.[43] Yet as recently as 1971, when the Synod of Bishops was to meet in Rome, some Catholics, even highly-placed, were opposed to the Bishops' even treating of this question.[44]

Indeed, many who survey the manifest problems which frustrate the relationship of the Holy See to the Church in the world at large insist that the Pope is insulated and prevented from a genuine understanding of the problems, if not by those who would protect a vested interest in the *status quo*, then at least by those who, out of some misguided sense of filial devotion, are loath to increase the burden on the

Holy Father's shoulders by delivering any reports which may be disquieting to him.

We could go on to observe that it is suppression that has created so many of the inanities—of either extreme rightism or extreme leftism—in the Church today. We could note that the contemporary Church is not unlike a teenage boy who is asked to run a four-minute mile when his parents have for years forbidden him to take part in any athletics. We could discuss at length the many things that should not be and that should be in the Church. Although that cannot be done with any justice in the present volume, limited in size and scope, let us make clear that it must be done, thoroughly and competently, and above all with genuine Christian love.

Of course the opposite can be chosen. We could decide to simply "drop out" in disgust and apathy. Or to tag along on the fringes of the Church without really understanding, let alone assenting to, what the Church is and is becoming. Or to pretend deep involvement in the Church, all the while befuddled by its vicissitudes, fearing to raise a question about anything because of the hangovers of prior censorship, devious punishment, ostracism which are deep-rooted in the Catholic experience. But to do any of those would be to ignore the challenges given us in the New Testament proclamations of the Faith, by the Apostles and by the Lord himself. It would be to ignore, too, the exhortation of Teilhard, who tells us that to affirm our existence is to deal with its problems, and that the only way to get past the whirlpool is not to circumvent it, but to go through it, to "shoot the rapids."[45]

So it means that, indeed, we cannot accept the descriptions of the Church as saving mystery (Vatican II), sacrament of Christ (Schillebeeckx) or Body of Christ (Paul) as mere theological niceties, and then go our own way. For if we believe those very theological expressions themselves, we are obligated to complete them by translating them from high-sounding truisms to fully-felt realities. This obligation remains incumbent upon us "in season and out of season, when convenient and inconvenient."[46] So it is that, in times that are perplexing for the Church and for ourselves individually, we demonstrate our faith in the saving resurrection of the Lord, present in the Church, by participating in the life of the Church, including its growing pains, even when it appears to fall ill.

We cannot understand fully Vatican II's reference to the Church as a mystery without understanding that, in that same first chapter of *Lumen gentium,* the Church is a pilgrim,[47] not yet having arrived at its final goal (as the triumphalists would have it) but striving towards it. To belong to and believe in the Church, and in the Risen Lord who is present thereby, is to share in the effort.

For Christ is risen. Our faith is not in vain.

1. At St. Anne's Parish, Fair Lawn, New Jersey, March 11, 1971.

2. This is the theme, well expressed, of the musical **Celebration,** by Tom Jones and Harvey Schmidt, which opened at the Ambassador Theatre in New York on January 22, 1969—especially in the title song.

3. "The Catholic Dilemma," CBS-TV, August 3, 1971.

4. Karl Rahner, **On the Theology of Death** (New York: Herder and Herder, 1965), tr. by C. H. Henkey; 2nd English edition rev. by W. J. O'Hara. Cf. pp. 32-50.

5. The Oriental rites seem never to have lost their emphasis on the centrality of the Resurrection. Cf. Godfrey Diekmann's article in the Proceedings of the North American Liturgical Week at Seattle in 1962, **Thy Kingdom Come** (Seattle: The Liturgical Conference, 1962).

6. So called because there was no consecration during this liturgy; I am referring to the Roman ritual prior to its revision in 1955 under Pope Pius XII.

7. I am using here the sort of theological language which has been challenged of late. For now, let us use it anyway, for the sake of its familiar

clarity, although we will investigate the question of situation ethics and ethical constructs later.

8. Hebrews 4:15.

9. The Church officially discredits such ideas. DS 301-303; 159; 166.

10. John 1:14.

11. The editors of the Jerusalem Bible, emphasizing one dimension of the meaning of sarx, note that "The 'flesh' is man considered as a frail and mortal being."—Alexander Jones, gen. ed., The Jerusalem Bible (Garden City, New York: Doubleday & Co., 1966), p. 147 (New Testament section), note "m."

12. Rahner, op. cit., pp. 57-66.

13. Cf. DS 3009-3020.

14. Luke 23:46. The Jerusalem Bible translation is used here.

15. Cf. Chapter 2, supra.

16. Cf. Matthew 19:27-30.

17. New York: Harper & Row, 1969. Also cf. Neale's chapter in George Devine, ed., New Dimensions in Religious Experience (Staten Island, New York: Alba House, 1971).

18. The translation used here appears in most English celebrations of the Byzantine Liturgy.

19. I Corinthians 15:20-23. Again, the translation is from the Jerusalem Bible.

20. I Corinthians 15:55-56; cf. Isaiah 25:8; Hosea 13:14; Revelation 20:14; Romans 7:7ff.; Hebrews 6:1ff.; John 16:33.

21. Cf. Rudolf Bultmann, et al., Kerygma and Myth (New York: Harper Torchbook, 1961), ed. Hans Werner Bartsch.

22. Cf. Acts 9:1-30.

23. Cf. Rahner, op. cit., pp. 56-80.

24. This is the foundation for Paul's doctrine of the Body of Christ, or as it comes to us today "the mystical Body of Christ." The term "mystical," not used by Paul, was introduced by later theologians to distinguish the Church from other types of bodies (moral bodies, physical bodies) and the term has remained in use through the present day, as in the teachings of recent Popes on the mystical Body.

25. Cf. Romans 6:3-11.

26. Cf. Rahner, ibid.

27. Acts 9:1-9.

28. Session here refers to Jesus being "seated at the right hand of the Father."

29. Again, "in-corporation" in the sense of membership in the Body of Christ.

30. E. Schillebeeckx (tr. C. Ernst), Christ the Sacrament of the Encounter with God (New York: Sheed & Ward, 1963).

31. Cf. George Devine, "Marriage—A 'Social Sacrament,' " in the Topic section of The Advocate (Newark, N.J.), May 5, 1968.

32. Schillebeeckx, **op. cit.**, p. 17.

33. **Ibid.,** pp. 47f.

34. I Corinthians 12:4-31; Ephesians 4:1-5:20.

35. John 15:1-7.

36. Walter M. Abbott, ed., **The Documents of Vatican II** (New York: America Press/Association Press/Guild Press, 1966), p. 14. (References to this work are for the cloth edition.)

37. Cf. George Devine, ed., **To Be A Man** (Englewood Cliffs, N.J.: Prentice-Hall, Inc., 1969), p. 141.

38. John Henry Newman, **An Essay on the Development of Christian Doctrine** (London: Longmans, Green & Co., 1897).

39. Cf. George Devine, ed., **New Dimensions in Religious Experience** (Staten Island, N.Y.: Alba House, 1971), Chapters 15, 16, 17.

40. Greeley has made frequent mention of this phenomenon in his syndicated newspaper columns.

41. **AAS** XXXV [1943], 193-248.

42. Cf. George Devine, **Our Living Liturgy** (Chicago: Claretian Publications, 1966).

43. Mandatory celibacy became prevalent in the Western Church, locally, on a piecemeal basis, synod by synod, place by place; it has obtained throughout the Western rites since the Second Lateran Council in 1139. Peter Abelard (1079-1142), a French philosopher-theologian, found himself a victim not only of the new rule of celibacy that obtained in his region during his time, but also of the belief that one must be a priest even to exercise such non-sacerdotal functions as scholarship and teaching in philosophy and theology. Thus it is that Heloise, his lover, is depicted as telling him that, for the sake of his career, she would rather be his whore than his wife, in Ronald Millar's fine play **Abelard and Heloise,** which enjoyed some success after opening in London in 1970 and on Broadway on March 10, 1971. Millar's play, based on Helen Waddel's novel **Peter Abelard** (London: Constable, 1939) is currently being made into a movie. It is a most powerful statement of many problems which affect the Church, and individual Christians within the structures of the Church.

44. Cf. **The National Catholic Reporter,** 22:7 (May 7, 1971), pp. 1, 10.

45. Pierre Teilhard de Chardin (tr. Norman Denny), **The Future of Man** (Evanston, Ill.: Harper & Row, 1964), Chapter III.

46. II Timothy 4:2. The translation has been paraphrased here.

47. Abbott, ed., **op. cit.,** p. 24.

Transformation In Christ

Those who have spent some time at or around colleges are familiar with the venerable traditions of initiation. Some ceremonies, over the decades, have tended to get out of hand, and not a few States have laws specifically prohibiting physical "hazing," thus making the fraternity paddle a mere ornament today. In numerous major universities, including my own, it has been decided that it is pointless and degrading for freshmen to have to carry cigarettes for upperclassmen, to wear special hats, and the like. But vestiges of initiation remain, in special groups or in whole colleges, as a means of ritualizing the entry of new members into a community.

Today, though the frosh hat and many demeaning initiation stunts are relics of bygone days on most campuses, there is a genuine attempt to make sure that the new students know their way around the campus, learn which courses to take and which to avoid (by means of formal evaluation or tried-and-true "grapevine") and which entrees to pass up in the campus cafeteria. And, even in an age that does not pride itself on its observance of time-honored ritual, it is usually made sure that the newcomers understand the traditions of the community they are entering, and that they will observe them properly.[1]

Suppose someone were to enter the scene with no "initiation" at all. He would not be forced to undergo ridiculous procedures and forms of harassment, as someone would have been a decade ago if he attempted to sneak by the initiation committee, but he would still tend to be regarded as someone whose arrival was incomplete, someone who was at a disadvantage personally, who didn't "know the score" and hadn't been through the same steps and experiences as his fellows. Somehow it would be felt that mere desire to be a member of the community, however powerful, would not be quite enough, that some official passage or entry into the group had yet to be observed and, perhaps, even officially recorded in some form.

A similar phenomenon is generally observed in religious groups. When the Jews understood themselves as a distinct race, culture and religious society, they acknowledged a common experience as prerequisite for membership: the Exodus of the thirteenth century B.C., wherein the Chosen People of God were delivered from slavery in the alien land of Egypt towards freedom in the Promised Land that would be their own.[2] But, of course, only a limited number of Jews partook of the actual Exodus in history; what was to be the way of initiation into this experience for the rest who were to come later?

One must be aware here of the force of what I call an event/experience.[3] An event takes place in history, but continues to be experienced throughout later history. Indeed, it is probably experienced more profoundly in later history than it was when it actually took place, since its results, implications, meanings, etc., are more profoundly understood. So, for example, the Americans who celebrate the second centennial of the Declaration of Independence in 1976 will have a more profound experience of the events of 1776, in one sense, than did the actual participants in the original event; those who celebrate the events of 1776 two centuries later will understand those events from a vantage point that was unavailable to Washington, Adams, Hancock, et al.

And all that is necessary to be "counted in," to share in the celebration of the Fourth of July, is to be an American. The celebration may be benignly observed by non-citizens who are friendly to America, but it is not the same. Just as it is not the same when Americans are pleased to sit on the sidelines when a British monarch is crowned or a prime minister elected.[4] What of one who *desires* to be an American? Unlike someone born in San Diego or Oshkosh or Baltimore, he did not become an American simply by birth, nor can he become one by desire alone. He must be, according to law, "naturalized," must renounce alien citizenship and become familiar with the laws and traditions of this country. Often, one who completes the naturalization process is more knowledgeable about some of these things than are some high school graduates who have taken American history and civics. But once the individual has gone through the necessary steps, knows what it is he is committing himself to, waits the requisite amount of time, becomes sufficiently familiar with his new homeland, he is "naturalized"; he is an American citizen.

So it became with those non-Jews who wished to embrace Judaism. These Gentiles had to learn the Law of Moses and the traditions of the Jewish religion and culture. But, also, they had to go through the same experience as other members of the Jewish people. Those who were born Jews had experienced the Exodus through the lineage of their forefathers, just as all Americans alive today, in a way, have "experienced" Bunker Hill or the War of 1812 through their insertion into an American posterity;[5] those who were not Jews to begin with, though, had to in some fashion be initiated into the experience on which they had "missed out." So it was that baptism (not an exclusively Christian ritual!) became the rite of initiation for proselytes, i.e., Gentiles

wishing to become Jews.[6] Those who had not been initiated
into the Covenant of the Exodus through the waters, either
in actual, historical fact or in the historic experience of the
people by lineage,[7] were initiated through the waters of the
baptismal ritual.[8]

Thus, when the Church became the visible manifestation
of Christ in the world, it became necessary that there be
some way of concretizing the relationship that men entered
into with the Trinity when they embraced the Gospel of
Jesus and its ramifications. For those who would share in
Jesus' death/resurrection, his teachings and mission, and all
of the circumstances and obligations thereof, there must be a
point of entry. Something that would not only signify the
initiation, but in reality *effect* it. As baptism for the Jews
was the point of entry into the central event/experience of
the Exodus/Covenant, so baptism is for the Christian the
point of entry into the central experience of the New Covenant, the saving death/resurrection of Jesus, son of man and
son of God. Paul explains this to his fellow Christians in his
pastoral letter to the Romans (6:3-11):

> You have been taught that when we were baptised in
> Christ Jesus we were baptised in his death; in other
> words, when we were baptised we went into the tomb
> with him and joined him in death, so that as Christ was
> raised from the dead by the Father's glory, we too might
> live a new life.

> If in union with Christ we have imitated his death, we
> shall also imitate him in his resurrection. We must realise
> that our former selves have been crucified with him to
> destroy this sinful body and to free us from the slavery
> of sin. When a man dies, of course, he has finished with
> sin.

But we believe that having died with Christ we shall return to life with him: Christ, as we know, having been raised from the dead will never die again. Death has no power over him any more. When he died, he died, once for all, to sin, so his life now is life with God; and in that way, you too must consider yourselves to be dead to sin but alive for God in Christ Jesus.[9]

The one who would follow Jesus, respond to his Gospel of salvation from the "human condition" of alienation from God, fellow man and oneself, will find in Jesus triumph over the most acute factor in man's situation, victory over death itself as we have come to know it. But Paul is obliged to make clear that this is not as easy as it might at first appear. For when a man dies, he can no longer sin; he is through with sin.[10] He is through living his life or being himself as a private entity; he no longer belongs to himself, as he is dead to the old life. But he is alive indeed; alive to the new life "for God in Christ Jesus."[11] This will mean not only a baptism as an isolated incident or ritual in time and space, but baptism as a way of life, as a continual dying to self and rising to a new life "for God in Christ Jesus."[12] However, the point of entry into this relationship with the Trinity is concretized, sacramentally, in Christian baptism.[13] And while sacraments are meant to cause what they signify, they are also meant to signify what they cause. In this regard, a brief look at the baptismal ritual commonly practiced in the early Church might help us to appreciate the meanings of this sacramental initiation:

The person about to be baptized usually descended three steps into a large chamber filled with water, and upon reaching the bottom of the chamber was encountered by the minister of the sacrament, who immersed the catechumen in the baptismal waters;[14] the newly baptized Christian then ascended three additional steps on the other side of the chamber, and often put on a special baptismal garment to indicate the putting on of a new identity in Christ.[15]

This ancient ritual clearly symbolizes the chief meaning of the sacrament of baptism: those who are initiated into Christ's death (shown by descending the steps) share also in his resurrection (shown by ascending the steps on the other side). Also, the passage from one side of the chamber to the other, through the waters, symbolizes a renewal of the original passage from slavery to freedom through the waters of the Exodus in the Old Covenant, thus a taking-part in a decision to leave behind the secure stagnation of the old situation (Egypt) in pursuing the hazardous but rewarding course towards the Promised Land. Thus, this sacramental point of entry is for the Christian a decision, as was the Israelites' evacuation of Egypt a passing of the point of no return.

The Israelite who accompanied Moses en route to Canaan through the desert accepted (if sometimes reluctantly) the delays and risks involved in the journey, including those stumbling-blocks which could never be anticipated. Similarly, one who accepts initiation into the life and death of Christ accepts, however implicitly, the risks and hardships involved in living that life, and dying that death.

It is often pointed out, today, that the first Christians to be baptized were adults who were converted from other ways (Judaism, the perfunctory observance of state religion in the Roman Empire, or the mystery cults which attempted to supplement the sterile experience of the Roman religion).[16] Thus it is presumed that, unlike the innocent newborn who is apt to be baptized today, the original Christian proselyte received extensive theological instruction and entered into his new faith-commitment only after having explored each and every possible detail contained or implied in the Gospel he was considering. From this premise, it is commonly argued that children should not be given religious instruction or baptized, but that they should be free to make their religious decisions and commitments from scratch when, upon achieving adult maturity, they can survey all the available options and choose without bias.

Whatever the other merits of the above argument, it must be pointed out that the history implied therein is incorrect. The early Christians were baptized after hearing and accepting only a skeletal proclamation (*kerygma,* in the Greek) of the good news of Jesus. It was only some time after their baptism and their living of the Christian life for a while that they became introduced to a more detailed and refined exposition of the doctrines and practices of the Faith (*didache,* meaning "teaching" in Greek).[17] The early Christians, inspired by the good news proclaimed to them, committed themselves to Jesus in his Church with enthusiasm, and later "read the fine print."

This situation was not without its problematic dimensions. While baptism is ideally supposed to signify an individual's death to the old life and to sin,[18] and was supposed to put an end to any dominion of sin over the new Christian, the fact is that many of the early Christians, often despite their own best efforts, found themselves unable to understand or to act in accord with all of the implications of the Christian Gospel to which they had radically committed themselves.[19] So it was that they had to receive numerous pastoral letters (most of them from St. Paul) addressed to specific situations in particular Christian assemblies, e.g., the divisive teachings of the Juda-izers that plagued the Galatians and Romans,[20] the superficial way some Corinthians had of observing the Eucharist as celebrating their unity in fraternal charity,[21] the danger that the Ephesians might not understand the meanings of the Gospel for human sexual conduct and Christian marriage.[22]

From the above, it should be clear that, just as one who had begun on another path was capable of changing in favor of baptism into Christ, the Christian, although baptized, remains capable of rejecting the Gospel and any or all of its dimensions. There is some argument today to the effect that baptism (or any other form of religious initiation) of any person, adult or child, violates the individual's freedom in that it prevents him from altering his position, changing his posture or reneging on his commitment at a later date. While such a change of stance is hardly envisioned when one is baptized, it remains a possibility, so that one who would choose to reject the Gospel remains as free to do so with baptism as without; however, one who would so choose, if he were baptized and to some extent educated as a Christian, would presumably be aware of the implications of the Faith in such wise as to appreciate the deep complexities that would have to be part of any decision in this regard.

So it is that, while the Christian is said to choose the way of Jesus once and for all in baptism, the fact remains that the choice implied is chosen and re-chosen in the Christian's life every day. Not to choose this day by day is to begin moving in the opposite direction.

Baptism, then, while it remains the basic sacrament of decision for the life of the Christian Gospel, is by no means a way of avoiding all further decision. Initiation into the ecclesial body of Christ does not bring with it the assurance that the Christian, once admitted to the fold, need never again face agonizing choices amid confusing alternatives. In fact, it will often be the case that, once one becomes a Christian, his choices will be less comfortable than they might have otherwise been, since he will be aware of the demands of the Gospel in ways that might well escape the "uninitiated."[23]

Among college students of late, there has been some grumbling that their parents have Shanghaied them, religiously speaking, by having them baptized (most of my student acquaintances are Roman Catholic, but I assume the same complaint prevails among others as well). They insist that their elders have chosen for them a way of life and a series of responsibilities, so far as religion goes, that they might never choose for themselves, and which they now choose to act contrary to. What is clear to me, here, is that the parents have exercised both a right and a duty to provide for their children's welfare as they best see fit (and as they often do in such matters as housing, nutrition, clothing, medical care and the like). Furthermore, the parents have utilized the freedom of choice which is theirs with regard to religion, initiating their children into the community of faith to which they themselves belong, effecting for their children a religious birth into a community which is not unlike a child's physical birth into the community of Galveston or Paris, of India or Great Britain, over which the child is never presumed to have control. It is clear to me, too, that the child, upon approaching maturity, is fully capable of rejecting provisions made for him as a child by his parents: he need no longer wear his raincoat during a downpour, need no longer take vitamins, is no longer compelled to avoid chills or various sorts of dens of iniquity, real or imagined. The child-becoming-adult is free to do as he will, regardless of any choices or provisions made for him in childhood by his parents.

But, some of my students would insist, this is not good enough. True, a child born into and raised as—say—an Italian-American Roman Catholic in Bayonne, or an Irish-American Roman Catholic in Jersey City—will carry with him throughout life an amalgam of experiences, attitudes, memories, visions and fears which are part of the indelible mark made on him by his religio-ethnic subcultural experience.[24] And so, the students would be inclined to argue, the individual's freedom of choice has been crippled from the outset. In this light, I would have to agree that these influences are not only there, but probably inescapable. But that does not mean they are insuperable when the young adult seeks freedom. In James Joyce's *A Portrait of the Artist as a Young Man,* it is obvious that Stephen Dedalus is as much a product of strict Irish Catholic upbringing as anyone could be,[25] but it is equally obvious that Stephen, albeit painfully, chooses to reject his Irish Catholic upbringing and identity. Today's youth are free to do the same, and I suspect that they are psychologically capable of rejecting the religious values of their parents just as they are capable of rejecting their parents' political or cultural values. To suggest that a youth has been bludgeoned into Roman Catholicism or Lutheranism or Methodism is almost as silly as suggesting that he will never be free to cultivate a taste for hard rock if his parents persist in watching Lawrence Welk on the family TV set, or that he can never vote Democratic if his parents have always registered and voted Republican.

Baptism as initiation, as decision, then must be seen as an ongoing reality, which does not terminate with finality at the end of a ritual action, but which is only begun and sacramentalized in that liturgy, and which endures effectively only insofar as it is reiterated by a series of choices throughout life.

We are led, now, to consider the second dimension of sacramental initiation, commonly called the sacrament of confirmation. At once the language becomes a bit confusing.

Does this sacrament serve to "confirm" that which was begun in baptism? To a large extent, yes. But to view the sacrament solely in that context would be to miss some of its meanings, as witnessed to by Christians and investigated by students of religion for centuries.

The difficulty involved in studying the sacrament of confirmation can be illustrated if we note that the ritual was often seen, in the early Church, as a completion of the initiation begun in Baptism, to such an extent that the two rites were often not distinguished one from another.[26] Furthermore, confirmation appears to have been carried out by different external rituals at different times and in different places, and this also has made it hard to trace the historical development of the sacrament in the Church's faith-life, although some light has certainly been shed on the matter in Pope Paul VI's *Divinae Consortium*.[27]

If it has been hard, as in the case of confirmation, to discern the nature of the sacrament with some clarity by studying its external from in liturgy,[28] another helpful source would seem to be the tradition of the believing and teaching Church. However, scholars are aware that even the documents of Christian tradition do not agree in all cases where the nature of the sacrament of confirmation is concerned.[29]

Some of the students in my sacramental theology classes have courteously noted the above factors, but have been unable to conceal the fact that they are not really interested in the questions involved. While I have no right to expect that every person in a given class would be enthralled by the *minutiae* of scholarship in Church history and related areas, I must point out that a real understanding of confirmation —which is much in the limelight of theological controversy today and has real implications for the lives of many Christians—cannot come without some appreciation of the myriad considerations which occupy the minds of theologians and similar scholars in evaluating the significance of the sacrament.

The notion of confirmation which has been most prevalent over recent centuries, and thus most influential in the religious experience of most of us, has centered in the Latin expression *robur ad pugnam,* implying that confirmation is a "bracing" for the hazards which the new confirmand is to grapple with in a hostile world. In this light, the "blow on the cheek" delivered by the confirming bishop was interpreted by catechists as a preview of the many blows that would surely be dealt us in the cruel outside.[30] The sacrament was often administered at or just prior to the time of graduation from grammar school. For Catholic school children, this was seen as a special protection by the Holy Ghost for the unfortunates who would not continue their education under Church auspices, but would instead be subject to the crypto-atheistic educational system of the secular Establishment. In any case, since confirmation came to be administered at or just before puberty, it was often felt that the Third Person of the Trinity had to enter the picture at that time, in a specially urgent way, to assist a Catholic youth in facing the many threats to purity that were to rise up during adolescence.

I do not mean to imply that there has never been harmful anti-Catholic bias in the public schools of some American communities (the existence of Catholic schools in America is a direct result of such harmful bias against Catholics), or that sexual coming-of-age presents no hazards to the individual Christian (indeed it does; more about that in Chapter 7), or that adolescence in general is not a time of problems when assistance is often needed (that this is so is a matter of public record). But I, and other theologians, would be a bit dismayed to see the idea of *robur ad pugnam* extended so far as to make the Holy Spirit's presence in sacramental grace little more than a spiritual and moral first aid, not unlike Popeye's fabled spinach. Indeed, it is perhaps an over-emphasis on the *robur ad pugnam* aspect of confirmation that has helped to prompt scholars to investigate further the historical background of the sacrament, and to discover and describe other possible meanings of the special presence of the Holy Spirit in this rite.

In this connection, various scholars in theology and liturgical history have argued, recently, that the evidence supports a view of confirmation as a completion of the initiation effected in baptism. They cite sources to indicate that confirmation was often the last step in the initiatory process of a catechumen to be baptized, and that the two rites (as mentioned above) often seemed to "overlap" in such wise that the distinction between them blurred.[31] If one were to agree with this point of view, he might further be led to investigate the historical evidence on the other side of the coin, which testifies to the strength of the *robur ad pugnam* view of the sacrament. Here it would be discovered that scholars are doubtful concerning the authenticity of the documentation concerning the *robur ad pugnam* notion, as to whether it represents an early and enduring facet of the Church's faith-life, or is an invention of relatively recent origin (in the Middle Ages).[32]

While the evidence in this question appears to be inconclusive as yet, it is already apparent that one cannot line up solidly in the camp of the *robur ad pugnam* view of confirmation, period. And if one is persuaded that confirmation is more properly considered as a completion of baptism, the line of reasoning follows to call for confirmation administered soon after baptism, before reception of the eucharist, and in most cases, this would mean confirmation of infants or very young children.[33]

However, there is still another point of view which has important implications both sacramentally, on theological grounds, and also pastorally, in the practical exercise of the rite in question. This view reflects the thinking of some contemporary theologians to the effect that confirmation is a deputation to service in the Church for the redemption of the world in witness to the risen Lord Jesus,[34] and a participation in the Church's function as primordial sacrament (*ursakrament,* in the German of Rahner)[35] of man's encounter with the Deity.[36] Advocates of this view would tend to see confirmation as the sacrament of Christian maturity,[37] and thus would argue for celebrating this maturity in ritual at a much later age than commonly observed today, e.g., around age eighteen or twenty-one.[38]

Though this sort of discussion may appear at first to be one of the duller aspects of the current season in ecclesiastical intramurals, it points out the great necessity of sound scholarly foundations and evidence for those who would argue a case of fact or practice in the Church, especially since the National Conference of Bishops must now set the age for Confirmation. It also has serious implications for the nature and celebration of confirmation, especially as this may affect the lives of young people.

Suppose, for a minute, that we take the former of the two alternatives to the common interpretation and practice as rooted in the phrase *robur ad pugnam.* To do so would mean, clearly, that the eucharist stands as the terminal point of initiation into the Christian community, that all else pertaining to entry in the Church ought be done before one is admitted to the eucharist as sacrament of unity in the final initiation. The immediate effect of choosing this alternative, of course, is the common observance of confirmation among young children. This would raise, again, some of the questions just discussed in the earlier portion of this chapter (and,

I suspect, the answers would not become very different). However, it would raise additional questions of no small import, one of which is the whole issue of whether the eucharist is primarily a *sign* of unity in the Church, or a *cause* of it. Surely it is both, but if the former interpretation (*sign* of unity) were to prevail over the other, in that only those fully initiated (baptized and confirmed) at the preparatory stages were to be allowed the final initiation (in the eucharist), would this not influence, most seriously, the ecumenical question of intercommunion? It is presently argued by some theologians and pastors that to allow intercommunion between Christians of different denominations is to help *cause* unity between Christians of differing faith-commitments; their opponents argue that to do so is to carry out a *sign* of unity under false pretense (however sincerely),[39] and this would ultimately be counter-productive. If we talk in terms of confirmation as initiation preparatory to the eucharist, how could we support intercommunion with other Christian bodies? To confirm is to specify even more precisely one's membership within a specific Christian body. And to confirm as a requisite for eventual admission to the eucharistic banquet is to mark a clear distinction of this particular Christian body from the various Christian denominations (in the vast majority of Christian denominations) which do not recognize confirmation as a sacrament, let alone a prerequisite for participation in the eucharist. Now, if we believe in the power of the Holy Spirit sufficiently to believe that he becomes present to the individual Christian in an especially salutary way in the sacrament of confirmation, we can surely believe in hope that the Holy Spirit can vault the interdemoninational obstacles to the divine mandate that all Christians be one.[40] Yet we must be aware of the ecumenical implications for any decision we as a Church might take concerning confirmation.

But now, look at the final alternative: confirmation viewed

primarily as sacrament of Christian maturity, ordination to adult witness in the Church, and thus celebrated as one is entering the age of majority (e.g., eighteen or twenty-one). As a liturgist, I already envision some possible celebrations of confirmation in the context of or in tandem with graduation from high school or college, or entry into such vocations as teaching, social work, the Peace Corps, etc. Also, I imagine liturgies of Christian choice and dedication for one or a few individuals in a high school or college student community, or in a similar group of young people, wherein they would freely and maturely choose Christ and his gospel and dedicate themselves to witness thereto, throughout their adult lives. However attractive this vision may be, it would have to be corroborated by sound evidence from theological and historical scholarship, and it is not yet definitely clear that that will be the case. In the mean time, there are some problems with this manner of celebrating confirmation which are immediately apparent to me.

The young adult is seldom totally free from parental pressure, and pressure from adult society in general. Would young adults by the score be "pressured" into a celebration of confirmation, largely against their will, in the face of offers of material rewards, threats of embarrassing the family and being cut off, or whatever? A partial answer to our question could be found if we could calculate the number of unbelieving young adults who attend Mass with their families every holyday of obligation and Sunday, or who have left the Church in belief and practice but are married at a Nuptial Mass to the tune of clinking coins in the newlyweds' nest-egg accounts. If we are to opt for a celebration of confirmation later in life than presently observed, how avoid such sham, however infrequently it might occur and however difficult it may be to detect?

Perhaps one solution would be to simply accept the "old

school" or "hard line" approach. To agree that the crises of faith undergone by most young adults are but transitory, and that those who undergo the confirmation ceremony at the school, or in the young people's group, will be glad they did in years to come, after the unrest within them settles down (just as they will be glad they went to church with Mom and Dad, or had a nice Nuptial Mass, or whatever). Some of the presumptions here may well be correct, in many cases, but that does not suffice to *make* them correct, and our foundations for the conduct of the sacramental life of the Christian community, and the individuals within it, should be built on far more solid ground than this.[41]

More viable solutions, it seems, would be, in the first place, to studiously avoid a routine practice of confirmation-in-groups for young people. In a number of parishes, this practice now exists for the first confessions and holy communions of young children. Rather than the mass experiences of first-confession-followed-by-first-communion for a whole class of children, many a parish is now opting for the parents and child to decide when the child is ready to join the parents in communion, and to appreciate the significance of this action, and not a few parishes also allow the child to come to the sacrament of penance when he feels a need for reconciliation or forgiveness after having alienated himself from his God or his fellows, but not before that, and often not before first communion.[42] Could not the same style be selected with regard to confirmation?

One immediately recognizes the problems connected with the administration of the sacrament of confirmation by bishops as ordinary ministers.[43] One solution to the problem, of course, is to consecrate more bishops, even create more dioceses (or, if you will, sub-dioceses) so as to meet the needs of the Church in myriad ways, not just with respect to confirmation. Another would be to recognize that the clergy, in the earliest days of the Church's life, consisted of bishops only, and that all others (priests, deacons) are but delegates (if not downright creatures) of the bishops. Accordingly, as the bishops have delegated parish priests to celebrate the eucharist,[44] or to exercise the faculties for the sacrament of penance,[45] or to perform other duties, why cannot they expand the existing opportunities to delegate priests who are not bishops to officiate, when necessary, in the sacrament of confirmation?[46] I do not presume to favor either of these solutions over its alternate, at present, but merely to suggest that the practical problem is eminently soluble. And it may well be worth the effort required, to maximize the possibility of a celebration of confirmation which would have genuine significance for those involved, with minimal risk of mechanical performance in a mere ceremony being tolerated in opposition to the interior will of the young confirmand(s).

Of course, there remains the possibility which, for young Catholics, is perhaps the most awesome of all: that the present practice of the Church will not change. This might take place because some scholar will make the contribution of evidence which settles the dispute, at least for the foreseeable future, in favor of maintaining the current customs. Or, more likely, because most dioceses or parishes will continue their present practice since no strong evidence to the contrary, in one direction or another, seems to be persuasive.

But whether or not there be change in the observance of the sacrament of confirmation, there are contained in all the viewpoints just discussed certain elements which all of us—but especially young adults—would do well to keep in mind.

First is the basic realization, the one factor agreed upon emphatically by all who have viewed the mysteries of the sacrament of confirmation, that the Holy Spirit therein comes to the individual Christian in a most special and helpful way.

If this seems but a truism, it should be pointed that today's Christian is like the fabled baseball team of *Peanuts'* Charlie Brown; he needs all the help he can get. The Christian of today, if he be typical at all, is probably much like the disciples in the upper room as depicted at the beginning of the Acts of the Apostles:[47] very much afraid of a world-situation rife with stumbling-blocks, contradictions and perhaps even direct and hostile opposition for the Gospel and the Christ which he has been introduced to and led to believe in. To believe in and receive the help of the Holy Spirit is to believe in oneself as a Christian and one's Church as a Christian community viable in the world. It is *not* to put on the falsely-smiling mask of giddy hyper-optimism, or to become a Pollyanna, but it *is* to lend credence to the possibilities for Christians and Christ's Church in the world as we find it; it is to incarnate genuine and radical belief in Christ and his Gospel message, and in our ability—with rigorous obligations—to make these visibly and powerfully present in our *saeculum*.[48] And when I speak of rigorous obligation, I mean that the Holy Spirit cannot be presumed upon to make a legal wizard out of the civil-rights lawyer who refuses to study his torts, or a qualified psychiatrist out of a sincere religious who had a summer course in psychology once, or anything like that. To witness to the presence of the Holy Spirit is surely to admit that we are in a way channels for the saving action of God; we also exercise this witness, though, by remembering that our own actions become a part of the divine mission, and that our own actions had best be worthy of that mission.

Secondly, we should remember that the notion of *robur ad pugnam*, particularly as ritualized in our lifetimes, however out of vogue it may be, at least currently, cannot be wholly without basis. To say that adolescence, or young adulthood, will likely pose many questions or difficult situations for the individual and his understanding of himself in relation to his beliefs and courses of action is to record a commonly acknowledged fact. Of course, it is possible to exaggerate this by insisting (as some preachers have no doubt done) that behind every tree there waits a communist, or pornography peddler, or dope pusher, ready to ensnare today's youth unless they arrive on time for every one of their confirmation ceremony practices. But to say that the help of the Holy Spirit, and the individual's belief in and receptivity to the life-giving Spirit of God, at this time in life, could be considered superfluous is foolish.[49]

Also, we should note that belief in or receptivity to God as he was seen by the apostles at Pentecost means for us, truly, many of the things that modern theologians have seen in the sacramental realities of confirmation: participation, as maturely as possible, in the Church's role as the chief sacrament of man's relationship to God, in the Church's mission to make real in the world the person, teachings, values and presence of Jesus. Regardless of any further ecclesiastical give-and-take about the nature and observance of confirmation, this participation will go hand-in-hand with a deputation to worship and witness in the eucharistic community.

After the original Christians had been liberated in the visionary belief and hope and the powerfully transforming love that came with the Holy Spirit, their program for the Christian life in the world was outlined in this way:

These remained faithful to the teaching of the apostles, to the brotherhood, to the breaking of bread, and to the prayers.

The many miracles and signs worked through the apostles made a deep impression on everyone.

The faithful all lived together and owned everything in common; they sold their goods and possessions and shared out the proceeds among themselves according to what each one needed.

They went as a body to the Temple every day but met in their houses for the breaking of bread; they shared their food gladly and generously; they praised God and were looked up to by everyone. Day by day the Lord added to their community those destined to be saved.[50]

Since that first century of Christian history, some incidental changes have no doubt taken place: communism (ancient Christian or modern Marxist) is more often than not rejected as a means of achieving social and economic equity; the Temple is no longer important for Christians, since their numbers are no longer composed almost entirely of Jews,[51] and the breaking of the eucharistic bread, most of the time, does not take place in private homes;[52] moreover, ours is an age when the presence of the Spirit does not seem to be most aptly expressed by miracles and signs. But the basic elements—faithfulness to the apostolic teachings, the communal brotherhood of Christians,[53] awareness of and responsibility for the needs of others, a prayerful, worshipful life centering in the eucharistic celebration—they remain as necessary and as viable a program for us today as for our predecessors. Let us go on to explore some of these factors, and our possible applications of them in the contemporary world.

1. For an example of a new-style student initiation "handbook," cf. Joe Bakes, **et al.**, eds., **Mother Seton's Diary** (South Orange, N.J.: Seton Hall University Student Government, 1971).

2. Cf. the annotated bibliography in George Devine, **Why Read the Old Testament?** (Chicago: Claretian Publications, 1966), for some back-

ground reading suggestions on the Exodus/Covenant experience.

3. Cf. Devine, **op. cit.,** p. 9.

4. My wife and I were in England for a week in 1970 prior to the election of Mr. Heath over Mr. Wilson as Prime Minister. The common language and other ties we felt with the British could not alter the fact that there were certain elements of their national experience which were quite foreign to us, particularly the way in which their political campaigns are conducted (the British would likely say the same of us).

5. In the same context of "racial memory," all Irishmen have experienced the 1916 Easter Rebellion, all San Franciscans such as myself, even if born after the actual event, have experienced in some way the 1906 earthquake and fire, and so on.

6. Cf. Bernard J. Cooke, **Christian Sacraments and Christian Personality** (New York: Holt, Rinehart & Winston, 1966), Chapter 1.

7. Cf. note 5, **supra.**

8. Cf. Cooke, **loc. cit.**

9. The Jerusalem Bible translation is used here, as elsewhere in this book.

10. Cf. Romans, **loc. cit.**

11. Romans 6:11.

12. **Ibid.**

13. Cooke, **loc. cit.**

14. **Ibid.**

15. Cf. Galatians 3:27.

16. John L. McKenzie, **The Power and the Wisdom** (Milwaukee: Bruce Publishing Company, 1965), Chapter 1.

17. **Ibid.**

18. Romans 6:10.

19. Cf. Galatians 1:6-6:18.

20. Cf. Romans 3:9-5:11. Also cf. Barnabas M. Ahern, ed., "The Epistle to the Galatians and the Epistle to the Romans," **New Testament Reading Guide No. 7** (Collegeville, Minn.: The Liturgical Press, 1960), Introduction.

21. I Corinthians 11:16-34.

22. Ephesians 4-5; especially cf. Ephesians 5:21-32.

23. Cf. Cooke, **op. cit.,** pp. 8-14.

24. Cf. Garry Wills, "Catholic Fact and Fiction," **The New York Times Book Review,** January 23, 1972.

25. James Joyce, **A Portrait of the Artist as a Young Man** (New York: Viking Press, 1964).

26. Marian Bohen, **The Mystery of Confirmation** (New York: Herder & Herder, 1963), p. 15.

27. **Ibid.,** pp. 16ff; also cf. **Origins** (NC Documentary Service), 1:13 (23 September 1971).

28. The study of external liturgical forms, far from signifying a pre-

occupation with superficialities, incarnates the sound theological principle **lex orandi, lex credendi:** the external celebration or manifestation of a faith-life in worship signifies the inner beliefs of that faith-life. (This also occurs when an inadequate liturgy incarnates an imbalanced theological perspective, e.g., the sorry liturgical experiences of the early middle ages reflected the lack of insight into ecclesiology and sacramental theology at that time, etc.)

29. **Divinae Consortium** does not go much further than to indicate Confirmation as a special giving of the Holy Spirit. The document does, however, make clear that ". . . the laying of hands on the candidates, which is done with the prescribed prayer before the anointing . . . does not belong to the essence of the sacramental rite." Cf. note 2, **supra.** Also, **Divinae Consortium** generally supports Confirmation as initiatory.

30. Scholars now tend to believe that, rather than a preview of the blows to be encountered in the world, the action was a sign of the **pax,** or greeting of peace, to be administered gently and paternally by the bishop to the confirmand. Some others see it as a symbol of a military commissioning. In a number of countries, it will be omitted in the wake of **Divinae Consortium.**

31. Bohen, **ibid.**

32. **Ibid.,** pp. 18ff.

33. **Ibid. Divinae Consortium** leaves the age of confirmands to Bishops' conferences in various countries.

34. **Ibid.,** pp. 18-19

35. **Loc. cit.**

36. **Loc. cit.**

37. **Loc. cit.** Also cf. Cooke, **op. cit.,** Chapter 4.

38. One of the people to advocate and implement this in pastoral practice was Fulton J. Sheen, when he was Bishop of Rochester, New York.

39. This was the position taken by a Presbyterian minister, Rev. Guy Walzer, on my radio discussion program "Contemporary Theology Forum," in 1968.

40. Cf. John 17:21.

41. Cf. fn. 28, **supra.**

42. Many parents, led to believe that confession was a prerequisite for every communion, or at least the first, have been scandalized by this newer practice. But even such reliably conservative sources as the catechisms and the canons indicate that confession is necessary before communion only in the case of mortal sin; most pastors and psychologists today believe that young children may be old enough to discern the meaning of the eucharist and to receive it properly and meaningfully without being capable of, or at least without committing, mortal (perhaps even venial) sin.

43. **CIC,** Can. 782.

44. **CIC**, Cans. 697-706.
45. **CIC**, Cans. 873-882.
46. **CIC**, Can. 782.
47. Acts 2:1; cf. also John 20:19.
48. **Saeculum**, from which come our English words **secular**, and its derivatives, can be translated as **world**, or perhaps more appropriately **time-and-place**, i.e., the time-and-place we are in as the world we are in.
49. It would also be, strictly speaking, heretical, as was Pelagius, who had taught that the grace of God, particularly in baptism, while desirable for salvation, was not strictly necessary for man, since he could achieve salvation—albeit with considerable difficulty—without it.
50. Acts 2:42-47, again from the Jerusalem Bible.
51. The first Christians saw Jesus and his Gospel as the completion of all they had learned and hoped for as Jews, thus not in contradiction to their regular Temple worship. It was only after official Judaism made clear the unwelcome status of Jesus' followers that those Jews who accepted Jesus as Messiah began to see Judaism and Christianity as distinct religions. Cf. Barnabas M. Ahern, "The Concept of the Church in Biblical Thought," in **Proceedings,** Society of Catholic College Teachers of Sacred Doctrine (SCCTSD; now College Theology Society), Vol. VII (1961), p. 36.
52. However, it is becoming a frequent occurrence that the eucharist be celebrated in small groups, often in private homes. Note the term "breaking of bread" and not just "eating (of) bread," indicating the special character of the celebration. Also note the argument concerning the definite article (**tou**) in the Greek text, where the phrase is rendered **klasis tou artou.** Cf. Oscar Cullmann, **Early Christian Worship** (Chicago: Regnery, 1953), tr. A. S. Todd & J. B. Torrance, p. 15.
53. In the Greek, **koinonia;** cf. Giuseppe Ricciotti, **Acts of the Apostles** (Milwaukee: Bruce, 1958), tr. L. E. Byrne, p. 77.

-»→[5]←«-

One Bread, One Body

For those like myself who have been involved in the liturgical renewal of the Church for some years, there has been a
certain amount of unpopularity in Catholic circles. In recent
years, we have been blamed at every level (parish, diocese
or wherever we have worked) for change having come too
quickly or too slowly, too radically or not seriously enough,
and so on. A decade ago, it was worse, and we were not only
looked upon with some disfavor, but also with genuine curiosity, if not downright incredulity. In those days, the bias
was all one-sided, though. A liturgical left-wing had not
really developed in the Church, only a right-wing which kept
insisting that we, following the encyclicals and instructions
of the Popes, were the left-wing! In the skirmishes that en-
sued, people became interested in knowing how it was that I
became so interested in liturgical reform, and particularly
in the cause of a vernacular liturgy in the Roman Rite.

The interest which I, and many of my contemporaries,
had in liturgy was probably due to the experience of a vernacular, congregationally-participated Catholic liturgy in
the Byzantine rite. As high school and college students we
were able to sing and pray the Mass in English each morning, en route to school, at the Jesuits' Russian Catholic Center of Our Lady of Fatima in San Francisco,[1] when our fel-

lows who were less fortunate, or less interested, knew only a Latin liturgy at which they were silent spectators. But this experience in itself did not cause me to be sold, a hundred percent, on the notion of the Mass in English as normative. Like many of those who would have been considered liturgically *avant-garde* a decade or more ago, our circle of friends tended towards a sort of gnosticism: we surely enjoyed the Byzantine liturgy in the vernacular, but also had studied Latin well enough to follow the Roman Rite Mass without serious difficulty. We could be part of the "in-group" that knew the myriad prayers said silently by the celebrant and only relatively recently made available to the faithful in their own Missals:[2] *Deus qui humanae . . . ; Quod ore sumpsimus . . . ; Offerimus Tibi, Domine. . . .* We could sing, and tell the difference between, *neum* and *punctum* in Gregorian chant. And I think that we wrestled inwardly, even subconsciously, with the problem of trying to enjoy the best of both worlds: the elegance of the Latin liturgy, which we—but not everyone—could appreciate, and the beautifully simple clarity of the Mass in English, which everyone could instantly apprehend.[3] In my progress towards a solid vernacularist position, I think the point of no return came at the North American Liturgical Week in Seattle in 1962.[4] About twelve thousand were in attendance at this largest yet of liturgical conventions, held in the arena facilities on the World's Fair grounds: priests, nuns and brothers of practically every diocese and order, and even those bizarre lay people like myself who were interested in liturgy. The liturgy in the large convention hall was a spectacle in the best sense of that term. All these thousands of Christians worshipping together in the eucharistic banquet to which we had been called by the Lord, whose resurrection we were bearing witness to. At one of the Masses, the National Choir of several hundred voices[5] led the congregation in singing, most beautifully, the words *unus panis, unum corpus:* one bread, one body![6] This most salient insight into the nature of the Church —that we were the one Body of Christ united in the one Bread of the eucharist—impressed me as being so centrally important to what we all were about that if only one person in the large assemblage failed to understand *unus panis, unum corpus* sung in the Latin, then it, and all the other beautiful prayers and hymns in our liturgy, should begin to be rendered in the vernacular tongues of the People of God as soon as possible.[7] To do this would be to act, most seriously and substantially, on *unus panis, unum corpus;* it would be to realize that if it were truly to be one Body of Christ in the one eucharistic Bread of Christ, we could not afford to be divided, whether by language, culture, walk of life or extent of formal education. We could not insist that only the Latin-speaking were first-class members of the Church, or that Africans and Orientals were inferior to the beneficiaries of European culture, or that the *Missale Romanum* had to be normative for the Church universal.[8] We had to achieve greater unity, and had to do it by way of developing our diversity.

So it was that much of the liturgical renewal movement in our time has come to be (if not at first, then certainly in its more mature stages) a concretization of the basic doctrine that those of us who partake of the one eucharistic Bread of Christ are one in his Body, the Church. St. Paul has pointed this out,[9] and he has also given us a vivid demonstration of the importance of diversity in the life of this body, when he likens the Church to a human body whose different organs each perform their own distinct functions, but *interdependently*.[10] Each of the organs depended on the others, yet made its own unique contribution to the life of the total body. And all united to the head of the Body, Christ. And this is largely what we celebrate in the eucharistic Bread, our unity in the eucharistic Body.

In 1963, prior to the widespread changes in the liturgy issued by Vatican Council II, Pope John XXIII introduced into the Roman Rite the practice of the celebrant, while distributing the host, saying to each communicant *Corpus Christi*, and the communicant replying *Amen*.[11] Or, as we render it in English today, "The Body of Christ. Amen." Is this prayer intended to witness, however briefly, to the real presence of the Body and Blood of Jesus in the eucharist? I am sure that it is. But I do not think that is the only "Body of Christ" to which we are giving witness in communion. I think we are also giving witness to that Body of Christ which is the Church itself, that we are signifying our membership and faith in the Church as the incarnation of Christ in the world. To be in communion with Christ, then, is to be in communion with Christ, *in* Christ, in his Church.

And to witness to the Church is not to witness or to surrender ourselves to a monolith. Diversity has always been a part of the Church's very life. As we noted above, a Latin liturgy was never universal in the Church (although many believed, or were led to believe, that it was). Nor has a celibate priesthood ever been . . . let alone Gothic architecture, black clerical suits, Bingo, Gregorian or guitars.

Some years ago, there arose a controversy over whether the eucharistic liturgy should be conceived of as a *sacrifice* or as a *meal*. Those who argued the former case noted that, traditionally, they had been taught about the sacrificial nature of the Mass and that, accordingly, certain liturgical proprieties had to be observed (the priest with his back to the people, facing the altar of God and mumbling the prayers *sotto voce*, and thus why not in Latin?) Those who insisted on the eucharist as a meal tended to regard the sacrificial concept as a bit old-hat (or, in their politest language, "preconciliar"). Thus it followed that the altar, no matter how obviously temporary or ugly, had to face the congregation and the permanent altar had to be done away with immediately; the communicants had to take the host in hand, not be "fed" it by the priest, and no one should ever allow himself to be or to look too serious during the festive banquet.

We are all too familiar with the sorts of extremes that have been visited upon us by ironclad insistence upon the eucharist as *either* sacrifice *or* meal. Of course, both extremist positions ignore the very diversity to which we must witness in the Church, and concomitantly ignore the fact that the eucharist is both sacrifice *and* meal.

Indeed, there are many facets of meaning and implication in the celebration of the eucharist which are important, and also interdependent. Let us explore some of them as centers of unity in the diversity to which we witness in the eucharistic Body of Christ.

First, to ponder the notion of sacrifice. The Mass is sacrifice indeed. The word *sacrifice* itself comes from the Latin phrase *sacrum facere* (to make holy). And our word *holy* comes ultimately from the Hebrew *qadesh,* meaning to separate or to cut off. The Hebrews expressed their religious experiences in the terms of their daily lives in the world. So for something to be holy was for it to be cut off, set aside for a special purpose or meaning, as with the holy place in the temple, or more importantly the holy of holies. Certain items or objects were designated as holy, and thus set aside from the rest, as were the members of the Levite tribe, the only ones who could perform the holy functions of a priest. When sacrifice was observed in the Jewish liturgy of the Old Testament, a victim was made holy, i.e., set apart, by its being offered to God. This meant its immolation (destruction) so as to render it useless to the people, so that they could not take it back for their own use after "giving" it in sacrifice to God. This was accomplished by making of the victim a holocaust, e.g., a sacrifice of wheat was burned, as was an animal after it was killed. In the case of either sacrifice, the smoke rising from the altar heavenward was seen as a symbol of the prayer of the people to their God. And in the instance of an animal sacrifice, yet another important facet of symbol became apparent.

The animal having been offered to God was now *his,* no longer the people's. Within the veins of the animal there remained some blood, before the holocaust was burned. Blood, then as now, was recognized as the basic *life-force.* So some of the blood was sprinkled about the altar, and the place of sacrifice where the people had assembled, to show that *God's life-force* was now being imparted to the people in response to their act of worship. God, pleased with the sacrifice of his people, now imparted to them his own very life-force, his own subsistence for his people.

In the Christian eucharist, the life-force takes the specific form of a *meal.* We are all aware of the fact that it might be possible for one to take all his necessary life-sustaining nourishment somewhat synthetically, e.g., by means of tablets or solutions (some people on diets do this, and it often has to be done, at least for a time, when patients in hospitals must be fed intravenously). But this is far from a normal way of nourishing ourselves, so far as we are concerned. We much prefer to be nourished in the context of a *meal,* and everything that we would commonly expect from a meal. I have often observed (and participated in) the hurry-up-fuel-up in the subway: a 37 cent hot dog wolfed down in less than a full minute three levels underneath 59th and Lexington, waiting to transfer from the IRT to the BMT. No one (I am convinced) really *enjoys* this sort of nourishment, but it often becomes the only available way of keeping the bodily organism fueled-up during a hectic day. This is surely a matter of necessity, as opposed to one of choice or preference. It's *life-force*, all right, but most people I know would prefer something more along the lines of a normal *meal*, even if the nutrients ingested be essentially similar. We might once more refer to the Old Testament antecedents to the Christian Covenant. The Passover meal *(seder)* of the Jews is a celebration of their identity as the People of God, saved and given renewed life in the Exodus. The eucharistic meal of the Christian community is a celebration of our identity as the People of God, saved and given renewed life in the sacrifice of Jesus as victim and priest, dying and rising that we may die and rise with and in him.[12] We could hardly imagine a devout Jew of today rushing up to the lunch counter in the subway and ordering a paper-plate Passover meal to be gobbled down before the next downtown express comes. Similarly, Christians partake of the eucharistic sacrificial meal not only to partake of a life-force given by Christ, but also to celebrate, as a community, our identity as the redeemed People of the Risen Lord in the New Covenant of his Death/ Resurrection.[13]

It is this consideration which further precises the nature of the meal in which we participate: it is a meal of *thanksgiving*, and that is precisely the meaning of the term *eucharist* (from the Greek *eucharistia*-thanksgiving). To be thankful means to participate in the celebration, and to participate in it as fully as possible. The gift for which we are thankful, here, is the saving presence of Jesus in the world, specifically in the sacrament of the eucharist, made available to us in the form of a life-giving banquet. To be genuinely thankful for the banquet as offered us means, certainly, to "take and eat of this," as Jesus has mandated.[14] Yet it is sometimes surprising how few people, proportionately, do just that. A large number of the people attending the eucharistic liturgy regularly do not partake of communion. In part, this may be due to some problems or misunderstandings within the Catholic community which have been alleviated to a large extent in recent years, beginning with the pontificate of Pope St. Pius X.[15] In his *motu proprio* of 1905, Pope Pius urged more frequent communion by the laity, just as he had urged more emphasis on the liturgy in his *motu proprio* of 1903.[16] His emphasis on lay involvement in the eucharistic liturgy—especially by means of frequent reception of communion—has been emphasized again and again by popes down to the present day.[17] Yet there are still some Catholics who feel that confession (even in the absence of serious sin) is necessary before each communion, or that the average lay Catholic is so unworthy of communion that the altar should be approached only rarely or for special occasions.[18] And yet the very nature of expressing thanksgiving for a gift implies making use of or partaking in the gift. Imagine a hostess putting out a beautiful spread on the table, and being told repeatedly by a guest what a beautiful meal it was, and yet experiencing the pain of seeing the guest eat none of it! She would have cause to wonder about the value of his thanksgiving. So too with Christians at the eucharist: to be truly participating in the eucharist (-thanksgiving) is to partake fully in communion.

We have spoken, above, of the presence of Christ in the eucharist. Here, some observations or clarifications may be in order. Perhaps the most important note to emphasize here is the fact that Christ's presence in the eucharist is not only a real presence, as it is properly called, but also a *total* presence. Thus, for Jesus to be really present—to be totally present—in the eucharist means to be present in his risen condition, as Lord triumphant over the limitations of time and space, as the victor over death. He is present in the continuing reality of his saving actions in dying/rising/ascending/sending-the-spirit. He is present in his totality as Lord of the New Passover. Accordingly, when we worship eucharistically we do not worship the dead Jesus on the cross, or the earthly Jesus whom we have come to know of in the Gospel narratives (to be sure, these are truly facets of the Christ whom we encounter and worship). But the Christ whom we do encounter and worship is the total Christ, not limited to his earthly ministry, his death, or any other single factor of his person and role in salvation. If we understand this, we begin to clear up some of the well-intentioned misunderstandings which have obfuscated much Catholic eucharistic piety. While eucharistic devotion by visits to the tabernacle remains admirable, we need no longer envision the Lord (risen and not subject to spatial limitations) as a prisoner in *need* of visitors. While the delegation of Christ's power to the celebrating priest is in no wise diminished, we need no longer envision the priest as some sort of a sacramental magician who "has the power to bring God himself down upon the altar" (as one bishop said in a sermon not long ago).[19] Rather, we think of Christ as the Risen Lord who renders himself present to us, in his totality, in the sacrament of the eucharist, in the context of the liturgy wherein Christ's ordained representative presides at our act of worship in receptivity to the presence of Jesus.

We have made note of the presence of Christ in the eucharistic liturgy, and of our opportunity to encounter him eucharistically. Yet, one may rightly ask, how are we to encounter Christ unless we know him, and how are we to know him? We know him by his deeds and words as he reveals himself to us, especially (though by no means exclusively) in the liturgy itself. In this connection, it is indeed fortunate that we have seen a recent rediscovery of the Service of the Word in our eucharistic liturgy. During the turbulent sixteenth century, Luther and some others among the reformers complained, with some justification, that the Catholic clergy was not putting proper emphasis on the ministry of the word to the laity.[20] While the Council of Trent, and some subsequent actions of the Catholic Church, tried to set aright the balance between liturgy-of-the-eucharist and liturgy-of-the-word, we have not begun to see a truly balanced relationship emerge until just recently, since the Second Vatican Council.[21] In even the years just before the Council's initial reform of the Roman liturgy, we heard the Gospel and Epistle proclaimed to the people in their own language as a matter of course only on Sundays and other holydays of obligation in most places, and a homily preached only on the same days. And even what might have occupied the place of a homily in those days could well have been a piece of oratory irrelevant to the liturgy itself, such as a fund-raising harangue. The years since the Council have far from erased all of the inadequacies in our ministry of the word—even with greater emphasis on preaching, and a greater diversity and depth of selections from the Bible in our liturgical readings. But we are beginning to notice a much more mature and fully developed stress on the lessons of God's Word in Scripture within our liturgical experience.[22]

However, to know Jesus in his proclaimed word in the liturgy, it is not sufficient that the word be promulgated with competency. It is also imperative that the word be *listened to* carefully. To listen carefully means to prepare oneself to be receptive to the lessons of the liturgy, and to contemplate them afterwards. It means, too, to study the liturgical texts, to whatever extent practicable, so as not to miss some of the insights therein. I am personally unhappy with the tendency to eliminate the proper prayers of the Mass (entrance antiphon, etc.) for hymns, because some valuable Scriptural components of the liturgy are being obscured here. I am not much happier when the proper antiphons with their respective psalm-verses are shortened, or when an oration (collect) is improvised in place of the liturgical text. A study of the actual prayers of the liturgy may be of great help and great worth to the individual Christian in his attempts to understand what it is that Christ would say to us, here and now, in our encounter with him in the liturgy. Let us make clear, too, that our prayers or hymns of response are part of the instruction which the liturgy provides for our understanding of our identity as members in Christ. For example, at Easter, when we especially celebrate the saving resurrection of Jesus, when we sing or say *Alleluia!* we come to learn something of what our joy should be as sharers in the salvific Death/Resurrection (Passover) of the Lord. This sort of reference should make clear some of the effort that is required of us if we are to listen well to what is said to us, even by ourselves in praising God, in the liturgy.

And if we have listened well in the liturgy, we are then ready to take into the world with us the presence of Christ as he has come to us in word and in eucharist. So it is that we concentrate now on the facet of *dismissal* in the liturgy. Our expression *Mass* comes from the Latin *missa.* The famous words of the Latin liturgy, *Ite, missa est* have been rendered in English as "Go, you are sent forth" or "Go, the Mass is ended." When the Roman Mass was first translated into English, the versicle and response at the dismissal were "Go, the Mass is ended," followed by the congregation's "Thanks be to God *(Deo gratias).*" The clumsy words implied, inadvertently, that the congregation was glad to be getting out of Mass, at last (perhaps this was not altogether untrue, in some instances). Now the English text of the liturgy seems more appropriate to the meaning intended: "The Mass is ended, go in peace," "Go in the peace of Christ" or "Go in peace to love and serve the Lord," followed by "Thanks be to God."[23] The implication, manifestly, is that we do not hoard to ourselves the riches of our ex-

perience of Christ present in word and eucharist in our worshipping community, but that we share that presence as
effectively as possible in and with the world we live in. There
will be myriad ways in which we can incarnate the liturgy
in life, each of us according to what we have received from
the eucharistic encounter with and in the Lord, in accord
with our individual talents and opportunities, and in light
of the needs and situations which we as individuals come
upon in the world. Here again, we must keep in mind the
image of the body as an organism of interdependent members, as mentioned by St. Paul.[24]

I like to envision this in terms of a bicycle wheel, wherein
the spokes all radiate outward from the hub to the rim, and
in turn inward from the rim to the hub. If all of the spokes
connect perfectly to the rim and not to the hub, or to the
hub but not the rim, the wheel cannot function, and is no
good. So with our membership in the Church: if we all connect to the central unifying force of Christ as head of the
body, hub of the Christian community, as present to us
sacramentally, but do not relate this to the world around
us, we fail as Christians. Likewise, if we are admirably concerned with the needs and situations of the *saéculum*, but
are not plugged into the central source of life and unity
which is Christ in the Church, we become dysfunctional.

It used to be felt by many a Catholic that one's own communion with Jesus was all that was needed. This type of
attitude was once parodied in a little song (usually sung to
the tune of the hymn "Rock of Ages"): "God's on my side,
just we two—and we have no need of you!" To exhibit such
an attitude is, of course, to fail to witness to the mystery of
Christ as present in the Church or in the world at large, to
fail to witness to the oneness of mankind as a race of brothers
and sisters having God as their common father. To a large
extent, this sort of attitude is being erased from Christian

spirituality today, and it is being realized that social concern is necessary to genuine Christian identity, as is personal spiritual development. The spokes are all becoming connected quite firmly to the rim.

But there can be another problem here: the connection of the spokes to the rim, but not to the hub. There has been a great tendency of late, especially among young people, to become socially involved to an extent which could well put many of yesteryear's Christians to shame, but this often takes place entirely apart from the Christian community. Several observations could be made about this. In the first place, one could certainly opine (as does Karl Rahner in his notion of the "anonymous Christian"[25]) that these individuals are indeed Christians doing the work of Christ and his Church, even if they are not conscious of the fact. But that idea, worthwhile though it may be, does not speak to the question at hand in its entirety. The phenomenon is also due, I think, to the fact that the Church is becoming less responsible, *as Church*, for the exigencies of the world. This can be, and probably is in practice, both a good and a bad thing.

The Church, particularly in America, has largely been forced into the context of a subculture. America is officially secular, religionless. Unofficially, particular religions may prevail in the nation generally or in parts thereof, e.g., a sort of nondescript middle-of-the-road Protestantism has often been described as the unofficial state religion of the U.S. In some localities, a particular religion holds sway to an amazing degree, permeating every facet of life, e.g., the Church of the Latter Day Saints (Mormons) in Utah. However, Roman Catholicism as a religious point of view or a religious group, much like Jewry, has never really taken such hold of the life of the community. Even in places where Roman Catholics have seemed to approach a substantial percentage of the population (e.g., San Francisco, Los Angeles, Northern New Jersey) there have always been enough "non-Catholics" to make the Catholics feel as a community apart, sharing in special hardships and special benefits, having their own ways of looking at and speaking about and doing a variety of things.

Thus the development of a Catholic subculture in America, with its own educational system from kindergarten through post-doctoral studies, its own hospitals and social service agencies, its own newspapers (an American Catholic daily, somewhat a rival to *The Christian Science Monitor*, is reported to have been contemplated at one time), its own youth organizations (CYO as distinct from YMCA/YWCA, let alone YMHA/YWHA), its own para-military organizations (Catholic War Veterans), insurance aggregations (Catholic Knights of Wisconsin, etc.), fraternal "lodges" (Knights of Columbus and Daughters of Isabella), movie rating systems (NCOMP, formerly the Legion of Decency), groups formed in response to social concerns (Catholic Interracial Council), and so on. This seems to have happened, not because Catholics have a mania for starting or joining organizations, but because Catholics in America were fearful (in some cases, at least for a time, rightly so) that the avenues offered them by the society around them would not suffice for their concerns, or would not be fair with respect to their own particular interests as Catholics. As observed previously,[26] Catholic schools were developed because Catholics felt that they would not be treated fairly in public schools which, for some time, suffered from anti-Catholic bias. Catholic hospitals were founded because the medical needs of Catholics might not be served otherwise. Hostility towards immigrant newcomers to America—Irish, Italian, Polish—made Catholics feel the need to band together, to rally 'round their Church, in ghettoes in many large cities (some of which still exist), and to take care of themselves and their own.

Nowadays, all of American life is far more secularized than before, to the extent that one's religious persuasion entitles him to no special privilege or disfavor, and Catholics need not be so wary as they once were of secular institutions (governmental or otherwise). Many of today's American Catholics feel that their children's religious education can be served without enrolling them in parochial school, and that they will not be made infidels by going to the public school. Many feel that their needs as Catholics and as patients can and will be respected by a gynecologist who is Jewish or a hospital which is Presbyterian. And, in some cases, American Catholics feel that they will fare better for going outside the subculture. They know that, because they have come from the out-group, they will have to be treated fairly, since no one would want to invite charges of inequity. One wonders, in this connection, if Jesuit congressman Robert Drinan would enjoy the same rights in many diocesan priests' senates or within his own religious community as he can in the U.S. House of Representatives, or if priest-sociologist Andrew M. Greeley would have as much leeway at some Catholic universities as he enjoys at the University of Chicago.

Part of this is the whole tension between what sociologists call *gemeinschaft* and *gesselschaft*:[27] in a *gemeinschaft* situation, where personal relationships and feelings become the coin of the realm, one can be in great favor or great disfavor because of who he is, how he thinks, etc. In a *gesselschaft* situation, noted and often damned for its impersonal objectivity, no one has to like or agree with an individual, but all must accord him his due rights. The modern American Catholic is now caught in a tension between the preservation of the *gemeinschaft* values of a religious community

and the *gesselschaft* values that would serve as some sort
of "insurance" when the religious community undergoes the
sort of turmoil that has been in evidence over the past
decade. Many Catholic institutions and structures are now
dealing with this tension in ways which in the long run
will prove healthy, but many of the Catholics affected by
those structures remain to be convinced. In any event,
secular institutions and structures (especially the State) are
now taking over some of the protective and organizational-
social roles which the Church used to have to play in the
American Catholic subculture. This means that the Church
of Drinan and Groppi and the Berrigans, for all its involvement in social issues, often appears less involved *as institu-
tion-Church* than did the Church of YCS/YCW/YCM, Car-
dijn and Suhard and Shiel. The individual Catholic today
often feels that his involvement in the *saeculum* can take
place without the Church, or even despite the Church, when
he finds that a good many of his co-religionists do not view
the problems, or their solutions, in the same way he does.

Some of the tensions we have described above, then,
make *institutional*-Church involvement in "secular" problems both less necessary and less apparent today than in
even the recent past. But this situation can be misread by
many people, especially many younger people, who tend
to feel that the Church should speak univocally on practically every situation from war in Indochina to busing in
Queens. These people are often a bit too young to remember that, not long ago at all, there was a time when the
Church *did* tend to speak univocally on practically every
issue, when there was (or was supposed to be) a clear-
cut "Catholic position" on virtually every question. For example, it was commonly held by Catholic theologians, hierarchy and laity in this country, as recently as a decade ago,
that a Catholic could not be є   from military service

on the basis of conscientious objection. Not much before that, it was felt that a Catholic had no business attending a secular college, for whatever good reason, or going to swim at the local "Y." Refusal to take the Legion of Decency pledge was considered tantamount to apostasy (although the Legion had little more official ecclesiastical status than the St. Helena's Parish Glee Club), and anyone who took the pledge seriously could never buy medications in an emergency from a druggist who had once offered *Esquire* for sale on his magazine rack.[28]

Our youth may indeed be seriously disappointed if the American Bishops have not resoundingly condemned government policy on Indochina, but they fail to see that many of the American Bishops, and the Catholics they represent, have felt otherwise, not because they are warmongers, but because they are so convinced as a matter of conscience, and are exercising prudence by not legislating their own view of this complex moral issue upon American Catholics, including our youth, *in toto*. So it is that today's young Catholic is free to enter the service *or* be a C.O., as his conscience would lead him, without undue pressure from his Church-institution (at least in most cases). He is not led to look to his institutional Church leaders in a paternalistic context, but rather to act as an individual Christian whose conscience and actions may differ from those of other sincere individuals in the community which is the Church.

Of course, to think and act in this way is to think and act in a way contrary to the old notion of the Church as monolith, and to thus invite one of two reactions: alienation or dialogue.

Alienation, practically understood, occurs when an individual (or group of like-minded individuals) feels that there is nothing they can do to affect an adverse situation, so they do not meet it head on. Neither moving towards an acceptance of or *modus vivendi* with it, nor stating forthrightly their objections to the situation, they attempt to ignore it, sabotage it, live their own lives in isolation from it. It is sometimes possible for those who are alienated to become so because of no fault of their own, due solely to the arrogance of their adversaries. Or for the adversaries to be guiltless, owing to the intransigence of those who become alienated (in which case alienation, as usual, is clearly a two-way street); more often, though, it is both of the alienated persons or groups who contribute actively to the situation.

It would be an understatement to say that alienation abounds in the Catholic experience here and now: some feel that Mass cannot be celebrated validly unless in an apartment, replete with dialogue homily and folk music; others that the liturgy can never take place properly outside a Church building, and that only the organ is the correct medium for worship-music. Some are convinced that a laicized priest is tantamount to the Antichrist himself, and others that any priest who "sticks with the system" is copping out. And so on and so on. When these groups or individuals studiously avoid one another, it could be said that, on the surface, much tension is avoided. In reality, tension is aggravated, since such isolation becomes fertile ground for caricatures, misunderstandings, downright untruths and calumnies about one's adversaries. And so it comes to be believed that all who sympathize with the Berrigans are communists, or that all who do not are fascists, and so on. Emotions tend to run wild in such situations of alienation, and the most bizarre positions and motives become ascribed to those with whom one does not happen to agree. That this is sorely divisive within the Church is self-evident.

The alternative to alienation, of course, is—if you will pardon a word that has by now been rendered almost ob-

scene—dialogue. I say "obscene" because one of the meanings of obscenity is that it occurs when the true meaning
or value of something is obscured. And if we have obfuscated
the meaning of anything over the past decade, it surely has
been *dialogue.* That is not because we have had (as some
would think) too much dialogue, but because we have not
had enough dialogue, at least not enough real dialogue.

If I attempt to understand your position, to appreciate
things within the context of your point-of-view, to evaluate
fairly what you are trying to say, I am on the way to effecting a dialogue with you, especially when you are willing to
do likewise for me. However, if I try to pretend that I have
no real position of my own, but am in complete agreement
with yours (when in reality I am not), we have no dialogue
at all, but a mere sham. If I pretend that I am older, younger,
more receptive or less receptive to change, than I really am;
if I pretend that this or that point, actually dear to my
heart, doesn't really make that much difference to me at
all, then I may seem to enjoy with you an innocuous and
polite encounter (and several cups of coffee and donuts,
such as have been in evidence at many a nice "dialogue"
session), but no real dialogue. To participate in dialogue, I
am obliged to speak as myself and for myself.

This does not mean that the obligations involved in
dialogue ever permit me to be jealous, boastful, conceited,
rude or selfish.[29] It does not follow that because I am attempting to engage in honest dialogue, I am therefore entitled to take offense or be resentful.[30] To do any of these
things would be to offend most fundamentally the Lord who
calls us all to manifest his charity to our fellows in the
Church and in the world.

Those of us who have read the Documents of Vatican II,
especially the Constitution *Lumen gentium* (On the Church),
know that the Church in Council calls us to dialogue with

one another, within and across the categories in which the document treats us (laity, clergy, etc.).[31] Those of us who have attempted to engage in true dialogue know, furthermore, that we are called to do this somewhat skillfully and sensitively, and that this takes practice and patience, lest we fall into the traps of alienation or false-dialogue.

Yet it is all eminently worthwhile, if we believe in the one bread and the one body of Christ. To not make that effort would mean to do violence to the very eucharist itself. But to make it would be to say a real "Amen" to the phrase, "Body of Christ."

1. The center was operated by the Jesuit Fathers, independently of their university and preparatory school in San Francisco which my friends and I attended. We had become interested in the liturgy there through a Russian fellow who was a student at the university and lived at the center. Eventually we developed into the English-speaking choir of the center, for liturgies held for English-speaking congregations. When the Russian people were in attendance, the liturgy was in the Old Slavonic of the Byzantine Rite. The principle of operation was that the language of the congregation (or the majority of the congregation) was to be used in the liturgy whenever possible (taking Old Slavonic as sufficient for the Russians). A widely circulated report, around 1959 or 1960, had it that Egidio Vagnozzi, the Apostolic Delegate to the United States, tried to intervene so that the Byzantine and other oriental rite priests in the U.S. who were under Rome's jurisdiction (as opposed to the Eastern Orthodox) would not celebrate Mass in English, since this might weaken American Roman Catholics' adherence (or subservience) to the Latin liturgy they had become accustomed to. According to the story, Vagnozzi was told by good Pope John to lay off.

2. Missals for the laity, now considered horribly passé, were a relatively recent development. As late as the nineteenth century, the laity were not allowed to possess the text of the Mass in translation, and for some time were not allowed to possess it even in Latin. Even when some relaxation in the previous discipline came to pass, the laity at first were not allowed to know the Canon, even in Latin, since this was a private prayer of such

a secret nature that only the clergy could be admitted into this **sanctum sanctorum**. This type of thinking is, of course, directly contrary to the theologically sound notion of the Canon or eucharistic prayer as the prayer of thanksgiving of the entire Christian community, led by their celebrating priest.

3. When interviewed by Rosemary Thielke for **Catholic Layman** magazine in 1964, I stated that a vernacular liturgy would require little education on the part of the congregation since the words could be understood at once,- as opposed to the veil of linguistic mystery that obtained under the Latin. It has since become evident that there are still many obstacles between the congregation and the words of the liturgy, but at least the basic stumbling-block of the Latin is no longer there. Cf. Rosemary Thielke, "The New Rites Can't Go Wrong," in **Catholic Layman** 78:4 (April, 1964), pp. 4ff.

4. Cf. **Thy Kingdom Come** (Proceedings of the North American Liturgical Week, Seattle: The Liturgical Conference, 1962).

5. The choir in those days was directed by Mr. Theodore Marier; it was later directed by Dr. C. Alexander Peloquin.

6. This notion is, of course, present in many hymns in common usage, notably "Father, All Thanks for Having Planted . . ." (paraphrased from the **Didache** of the first century, by F. Bland Tucker, 1941, alt., generally utilizing a melody attributed to Louis Bourgeois, 1543 (**Rendez a Dieu**) and "At that First Eucharist . . ." (William H. Turton, 1881, alt., based on the melody **Unde et Memores**, William H. Monk, 1875, alt.).

7. While many, if not most, of the members of the Liturgical Conference and those at the 1962 "Week" felt this way, it was not permissible to say so officially or publicly. The Vernacular Society was denied a meeting room on the premises at Seattle, and when they decided to have a "rump session" anyway, on the periphery of the "Lit Week," the Liturgical Conference press headquarters issued releases, handbills, etc., emphasizing that the Vernacular Society had nothing to do with the Liturgical Week or Liturgical Conference, and was not being recognized or tolerated thereby, even though nothing to stop them could be or was being done. The attempt here was to avoid offending the American hierarchy, who were considered unsympathetic to vernacular liturgy. Indeed, at the Liturgical Week in 1956, Dr. Joseph Evans of Chicago, a leader of the Vernacular Society, had given a talk asking that the hierarchy take steps to provide an English liturgy, and the directors of the Conference, next day, felt themselves obliged to make a public apology to the hierarchy for Dr. Evans' address. However, less than two years after Seattle, Vatican Council II, **not without the help of the American bishops**, had passed the Constitution **Sacrosanctum Concilium** ("On the Sacred Liturgy") initiating the use of the vernacular

in the Roman Rite. In fact, at the 1963 "Week," host-Archbishop John Krol of Philadelphia spoke to the assembly and noted that "the Church has acknowledged the bilinguality of the Latin liturgy." His remark indicated a progress which we would surely consider minimal today, but it was quite a development over the atmosphere of 1956 and 1962. Cf. **The Renewal of Christian Education** (Proceedings of the North American Liturgical Week, Philadelphia: The Liturgical Conference, 1963), p. 57.

8. As had practically been the insistence of Pepin in 754, when the Roman Rite was to replace the Ambrosian Rite outside of Milan, the Mozarabic Rite outside of the crypt of the Cathedral of Toledo, and the Gallican and Celtic rites everywhere. Cf. Josef Andreas Jungmann (tr. R. Brunner, rev. C. Reipe), **The Mass of the Roman Rite (Missarum Sollemnia,** one-volume edition; New York: Benziger Brothers, Inc., 1959), p. 56.

9. I Corinthians 10:17.

10. I Corinthians 12:4-31.

11. The formula used to involve only the celebrant, who upon distributing each host was to say **Corpus Domini nostri Jesu Christi custodiat animam tuam in vitam aeternam. Amen.**

12. Romans 6:3-11.

13. Cf. Chapter 3, **supra.**

14. Matthew 26:26; Mark 14:22; Luke 22:19.

15. Pope Pius X is called "The Pope of the Holy Eucharist."

16. Cf. Jungmann, **op. cit.,** pp. 120-121.

17. **Ibid.**

18. In the middle ages, it was common practice for the laity to receive communion no more often than annually, usually at Easter, and always outside of the "priest's" Mass. Cf. my brief treatment in **Our Living Liturgy,** p. 15.

19. Sermons like this are often given.

20. Cf. Jungmann, **op. cit.,** pp. 100ff.

21. **Ibid.;** Devine, **Our Living Liturgy,** pp. 15-22.

22. **Ibid.**

23. The Liturgical Commissions, The Archdiocese of New York, the Diocese of Brooklyn and the Diocese of Rockville Center, comp., **A Handbook for the Revised Roman Liturgy** (New York: ad usum privatum, 1970), p. 17.

24. I Corinthians 12:4-31.

25. Cf. Karl Rahner, **Nature and Grace** (London: Sheed & Ward, 1963), tr. Dinah Wharton, chs. 1, 2, 3, 5.

26. Cf. Chapter 4, **supra.**

27. Cf. Talcott Parsons, **The Social System** (Glencoe, Ill.: Free Press, 1951).

28. The Legion of Decency, though revered throughout Catholic America and funded by the Bishops, was essentially not an official organ of the Church as such. I feel it is not unfair to say that its importance was exaggerated.

29. I Corinthians 13:4-5.

30. Loc. cit.

31. Cf. Walter M. Abbott, ed., **The Documents of Vatican II** (New York: America Press, Association Press and Guild Press, 1966).

·•[6]•·

Alienation and Reconciliation

Until now we have spoken of Christianity and Christians in what might appear to be somewhat idealistic terms. We seem to have taken with the utmost seriousness St. Paul's remarks that once a man dies with Christ to sin and death in baptism, he is finished with sin once and for all.[1] The Christian, ideally, is one who has renounced with finality those values, orientations or actions that are contrary to the demands of the Gospel in charity and justice, that would offend his God or his fellow man.[2] Yet we know that Christians do, in fact, sin. We do harbor attitudes or perform actions, however occasional or seemingly insignificant, that take us away from the God who is all love and from our fellow men in whom Christ is present.

Sin is a matter which is difficult to view in a balanced perspective. When I was doing the "Contemporary Theology Forum" series on the radio,[3] I once interviewed a college chaplain and a pair of undergraduates from two different Catholic colleges in the New York metropolitan area,[4] in a discussion on confession. The question came up, "Why is it that today's college students seem to frequent the sacrament of confession much less than their elders?" The answer given was that today's college students don't believe that they sin . . . or at least not to the extent that calls for regular confession.

To a large degree, they may have something there, though it will be hard for their elders to see it. Even those of us who are just over thirty will remember that our childhood experience was rife with the possibilities of sin. Every possible sin, it seemed, was described to us in the earliest years of our lives. We knew that we should not commit adultery long before we knew what adultery was or had the ability to commit it. We were allowed to believe that every imperfection on our part was, however incidental or accidental, a probable sin, although fortunately only a venial sin. And the atmosphere of sin-and-punishment was present in our lives far beyond the proper arena of moral rights and wrongs. We often believed that failure to remember our answers in school (especially Catechism) could possibly be a sin (not using to the full and proper extent the talents God had given us). Surely normal sexual curiosity, leading to the asking of normal questions and the seeking of correct answers, teetered on the brink of "dirty thoughts" and "dirty talk," and thus sins against the sixth commandment. Any hesitancy to comply with orders or requests of parents, teachers or others in authority put us in danger of violating the fourth commandment. And any misfortune that befell us in the course of childish mischief was likely to be greeted with a reproachful "See, God punished you!" In fact, I knew a lady who, although with a bit of mock seriousness, must have traumatized her children forever by repeatedly announcing: "You left food on your plate; that is a *mortal sin* in this house!" (The same admonition, I learned later in life, would be applied to an adult who left a few drops of bourbon in his glass, though this occurred far more rarely, and the psychological effect was much less significant.)

Our lives as children, then, tended to be lived within rather definite lines of demarcation. To a certain extent, I insist, this was helpful. We knew that we were to avoid certain hazards (although we didn't always understand why) and that we had certain obligations to ourselves and to others (which we had yet to comprehend maturely), so that if we did pretty much as we were told, we would not be likely to get into too much trouble. Unfortunately, though, it got to the point where it was being carried too far. And generation after generation of us grew up wondering whether or not it was a sin (and if so, venial or mortal) to see *The Song of Bernadette* at the same movie house that had once exhibited *The Outlaw* with Jane Russell, or to sit in the back pew and observe the wedding of a Protestant business associate (one hardly had Protestant *friends,* in those days). We seemed to see ourselves sinning practically all the time, although I am sure we sinned far less often than we imagined.

In light of the above, it is not difficult to understand a reaction against this, not only on the part of today's young people, but *a fortiori* on the part of those who have been giving them their religious instruction of late. Today's youth —or his religion teacher—simply will not believe that as many opportunities to fall into sin could plague us as we had been allowed to believe. Today's youth is more likely to take into account the fact that, when you look at it, he has *not* killed, committed adultery, stolen, borne false witness or coveted his neighbor's wife or goods. Consequently, he wonders, why the big sweat? To some extent, this attitude seems to embody almost a kind of healthy innocence. Unfortunately, it can gravitate towards the extremes of naïvete and laxity. How can we keep a balanced notion operative in this regard?

First, we would do well to understand that, as implied in the Pauline theology of baptism,[5] the neophyte Christian (whether adult convert or infant) is sinless. Even the adult convert who may have led a life of sin has now died to that life, turned his back on it, finished with it, and begins a new life in Christ.[6] A Christian starts afresh in the life of love and grace in Jesus. It is legitimate to presume that a Christian has not reneged and does not renege on his Christian identity and commitment, until and unless he demonstrates otherwise. It was this principle which led the early Church to observe the sacrament of penance only very rarely, in the case of Christians who had fallen seriously short of the mark by way of a serious offense against God and man, and who wished to be reconciled to the community from which they had excommunicated themselves.[7] As a result, most Christians, in early times, never had occasion to participate as penitents in the sacrament of reconciliation (penance).[8] It is in line with this ancient Christian way of thinking and acting that many pastors and religious educators, today, have done away with the practice of "first-confession-before-first-communion" for children.

Some years ago, a number of priests who were fellow students with me in the theology program at Marquette brought up the question of confession for children. One priest expressed his gratitude for the fact that the prayers of the sacrament were in Latin,[9] saying "This way, I simply give the child a blessing, and omit the absolution, and no one knows the difference!" Why, I asked him, would he want to do that? "Because," he replied, "I can't find any sins to absolve!" The other priests present agreed that, in general, most children who come to confession have not really sinned, and are stretching their tortured consciences to find enough things to tell Father, such as the fact that they might have fallen asleep while saying their night prayers in bed, or been distracted during Mass, or some such thing. And of course, there is always the story of the boy who confessed that he had committed adultery. When the priest questioned the nine-year-old, it was learned that his "impure act" consisted of his failure to wash his hands after going to the toilet. So now there is the tendency—in general a healthy one, and

one consonant with authentic Christian practice "in the beginning"—to have recourse to the penitential sacrament only
as needed, and not as a matter of frequent routine. However,
certain questions remain.

First of all, what about the danger that, perhaps in over-
reacting against the excesses of the previous orientation
many people today will tend to ignore or minimize their
shortcomings and even their serious offenses against God
and man? This is a very real danger. Some popular theologians today, sometimes by misinterpreting or misapplying
psychological theory, are leading many Catholics to believe
that practically no one ever really sins. This type of misun-
derstanding can obviously lead to an individual's feeling that
practically everything he does is all right and needs little or
no scrutiny or effort towards improvement.

One manifestation of this is the tendency to believe that
"nothing is a sin unless you personally feel it to be a sin;
then it's a sin." Some people are no doubt sincere in saying
this. But it can easily lead to excusing the most unloving and
selfish actions by rationalizing in favor of ourselves, which
we human beings are quite able to do. This attitude is no
more healthy than that of the child of yesteryear who saw
sins every five minutes. It can lead to the mistaken notion
that I have no obligations to myself, my fellow men or my
God unless I freely perceive and freely choose to recognize
such obligations. In this context, the role of the Gospel as
a moral guide is effectively neutralized, since it can always
be argued that the Gospel, as it is transmitted through a
Church organization, is a tool of authoritarianism that has
no business imposing itself on the consciences of the Saved.

In this connection, we are seeing today many misunderstandings concerning the approach commonly called "situation ethics." Contrary to popular belief, the situational view
of ethics is by no means new or revolutionary. Christian

moral theology and ethics have *always* taken into account the situations surrounding human actions and possibly affecting their moral significance and the responsibilities of the individual(s) involved.[10] But the crux of the argument over situation ethics as it is expressed today has to do with whether anything, any human action, can be ethically or morally wrong *itself*, so as to allow us to say that this particular action should *never* be performed by *anyone*, regardless of circumstances.[11] In arguing for the situationalist position on this issue, Joseph Fletcher makes it quite clear that practically any description of an action will tend to involve a description of circumstances, and that it is indeed difficult to speak of an act as isolated from its circumstances.[12] However, Fletcher explores the question, in his *Commonweal* debate with Herbert McCabe, by taking situations involving actions commonly believed to be always wrong in themselves, e.g., adultery: may a woman in a prison camp justifiably commit adultery in order to save the life of her husband, or in order to be reunited with him, or to achieve some other obvious good for herself and other persons?[13] Here, Fletcher would argue, the norm "adultery is always wrong and prohibited" will not solve the dilemma, and another norm must be employed. What norm? For Fletcher, "Love is the only measure"[14] of the moral rightness or wrongness of human actions: actions which are loving actions (people are loved, objects are used) are good; actions which are non-loving or hateful actions (people are used, objects are loved) are evil.[15]

Father McCabe agrees with Fletcher that love should be the supreme measure of an action's moral rightness or wrongness, and that this is a fundamental principle of the Christian Gospel message.[16] But he must ask the question: "How do I *know* my action, in a particular instance, is a loving—and therefore morally good—one?"[17] Or, as I would ask the

question, "How do I know that my action is an effective incarnation of Christian love?" And to illustrate some of the
implications of my question, let us study momentarily the
character of Steiner in Fellini's famous film *La Dolce Vita*.
Steiner was pictured as one of the few individuals who remained at all human in the crazy world of alienated people
in *La Dolce Vita*. He had a wife and children whom he
dearly loved, and whom he did not want subjected to the
madness around them. So, in order to deliver them from
this hell-on-earth, Steiner killed them, and then himself.
Let us assume that Steiner's motivation was indeed sincere.
Let us further assume that he operated under tremendous
pressure in the situation of *La Dolce Vita*, pressure so great
as to suffice for derangement. Let us therefore assume *no
personal moral guilt* on the part of Steiner for his action (or
as we would say in traditional theological language, no subjective or formal sin). Does this mean that Steiner's action
was morally good—not in the sense that his own motivations
were good, but *in the sense that this type of action should
be endorsed or imitated?*

It may immediately be said that no other individual will
ever find himself in circumstances identical to those of
Steiner in *La Dolce Vita*. Probably, that is quite true. In fact,
all human experiences and circumstances are truly unique.
However, human situations often enjoy enough similarity
(all births, all deaths, all first loves, all homecomings, etc.,
have such a general similarity to each other that they can be
described by these very generic terms) that they can be
imitated or not, endorsed or not for others who will come
later, as "the thing to do" or "the thing not to do." So that
we can say that a particular type of action, *in general,* is or
is not worthy of emulation.[18] Thus we cannot simply say
that Steiner's situation is so awfully unique as to defy its
classification as a moral action *in itself,* i.e., in the objective

order, apart from whatever mitigating circumstances might arise from the psyche or surroundings of Steiner.

I would think that, if we gave sufficient thought to the question, we would generally agree that taking the lives of one's wife and children is, at least in general, not a good thing to do, circumstances notwithstanding. And I suspect that most of us would be quite willing to make this a principle, however implicit, for the conduct of our lives, and perhaps even those of others as well.[19]

So we *are* led to talking of objectively right or wrong moral actions, all the while admitting that circumstances may diminish or even eliminate personal (subjective) moral responsibility or guilt for an objectively wrong action.

And so it is by no means illegitimate to speak of moral norms for conduct. Within a Christian context we speak to the norm of fully human conduct in terms of the person and Gospel of Jesus. Yet we realize how difficult it is to discern the moral options that Jesus would have his followers take.

One of the points being made with some validity by contemporary moral theologians is that Jesus' remarks as recorded in the Gospels are topical, in so far as he addressed himself to the questions of the day when he preached. So it is that the recorded teachings of Jesus in the New Testament say nothing to us, at least nothing direct or explicit, about the Indochina war, the Middle East crisis, the moral issues involved in racial segregation, or whether the United States should legalize marijuana. Rather, the Gospels and other literature of the New Testament offer us two types of moral teaching: first, general principles (as in the Sermon on the Mount)[20] which will be applicable at all times in all places, and secondly, specific discourses on particular questions (such as "Render unto Caesar . . .")[21] which touch upon the life and times of Jesus' immediate environs during

his earthly ministry. Some of these may apply to our own
age as well, either in their original form, or with some obvious and understandable adjustment (e.g., the picturesque
expression "Caesar," in the above example, would be read
by us as "the Government").

Even those who had to interpret and apply Jesus' teachings immediately after his earthly ministry admitted their
difficulties. On some points, St. Paul could be quite clear
in applying the demands of the Gospel to the situations of
his contemporaries in the first century A.D.[22] But in some
other cases, he had to admit: "On this I have no word from
the Lord"[23] when asked for moral guidance. However, the
lack of a definitive mandate from the Deity did not render
Paul silent on the moral questions of his time. Even if he
had "no word from the Lord"[24] he often found it necessary
to reply to the questions put to him by the people who
trusted his moral and religious leadership, and he was careful to distinguish between teachings that came from the
Lord and those that were Paul's own.[25]

Paul was one of the first great Christian leaders in the
history of the Church, and his position is in a way a prototype of the position of the Church at any time in history.
In some matters, there is a clear teaching from the Lord. In
some others, no teaching seems evident (and perhaps none
is really needed). In still some others, the serious nature of
the problem necessitates a moral pronouncement by the
leadership of the Church applying the principles of the
Christian Gospel, aware of the inadequacies of the Church's
human leaders and their dependence on divine guidance.

It is obvious what sort of thing is involved in the first
area, e.g., the clear-cut prohibitions which are contained in
the Decalogue, such as "You shall not steal."[26] But even
then, it is necessary to determine what actually constitutes
stealing and what does not, and whether or how restitution

ought be made. Some of the positive commandments in the Decalogue, e.g., "Remember the Sabbath day and keep it holy"[27] seem clear too, but we must decide what the Lord's day is; in the Old Testament, it was the Sabbath (Saturday), but in the New Testament it became Sunday, and now the observance of Sunday, for Catholics in many places, may take place on Saturday (and with this latest development, many Catholics—including some prelates—are beginning to ask, "Well, then, why not Tuesday or Friday?"). It is just about as obvious that a contemporary interpretation of "Render unto Caesar . . ." obliges one to pay his income taxes, but even here, the issue becomes complex. Many Christians now feel that they must withhold part or all of their tax payments if their government—in their eyes—uses tax monies for immoral purposes, whether this be for the conduct of a war in Southeast Asia by the U.S. Government or the providing of abortion information and assistance by the City of New York, or whatever it may be that offends the conscience of the individual American who is Christian (or strongly motivated by some other religious or moral persuasion). And it need hardly be emphasized that today's Christians are faced with moral dilemmas even greater and more confusing than any of those alluded to so far.

The leadership of the Church, while recognizing and respecting the inviolability of the individual conscience,[28] attempts to deal with such problems and instruct the Christian community on them. But there has been much unrest and debate of late, concerning the way in which this has been taking place in the Catholic Church.

While many Protestant denominations have been accused of not providing enough guidance for their congregations on specific moral issues, the Catholic Church, at least recently, has been accused of over-teaching, over-preaching and over-legislating. To some extent, the accusation is not without basis, if not with regard to the official moral teaching of the Church, then surely with regard to the many popular understandings of morality which have become part of the "folk-Catholicism" subcultural experience,[29] e.g., some of the exaggerations of moral dicta which we described earlier in this chapter. It has appeared to many that the Church has always had a ready answer on hand for every possible situation before it could conceivably arise, as indicated by the numerous moral prescriptions tailored to fit hundreds of exigencies in the old moral theology manuals.[30] It is not surprising, especially in light of the fresh atmosphere ushered in by and since Vatican II, that a great many Catholics —especially young ones—would tend to react negatively to the excessively legalistic approaches to morality which they had come to know and be impatient with.

And it should not be surprising to see the pendulum swing to the other extreme for a while. So it is, often, that the college student who was frightened to death with the possibility that every natural sexual desire would be a mortal sin against the ninth commandment might now feel no qualms about engaging in sexual intimacies with a variety of partners . . . all of whom sing together in the same folk-Mass. And so it is that the young person who was drilled into never missing Mass under pain of mortal sin may likely stay away from Mass for a couple of years. I am by no means suggesting that anything—including a poor job of religious education or a legalistic approach to moral training—could really excuse or justify one's failure to worship with regularity, or failure to express relationships in a way which enhances and not devalues the worth of sexual symbols. Nor do I feel that much of the rebelliousness of today's young people is directly attributable to an overreaction against previous rigorisms in religion and morals. Much of it, I feel, is a direct result of the excessive pseudo-permissiveness which has become the hallmark of too many religious educators, in recent years, whose ego anxieties compel them to seek popularity rather than the satisfaction of having treated matters frankly and fairly. To illustrate: it has often enough happened, of late, that the students in many Catholic schools or religion classes are really not that interested, to begin with, in rebellion against parental or religious or civil authority, or in exhibiting the latest unconventional styles in clothes or grooming, or in proclaiming the "sexual revolution." But in many cases their teachers are passionately interested in these things. And when one considers the fact that these teachers of religion are often present or former clerics and religious-order members, one is inclined to wonder if this sort of thing is not largely a rebellion against the authoritarianism and sexual repression (real or imagined) which have made their marks on the psyches of the teachers.[31]

But whatever the cause of it, the failure to take seriously enough the fact that we *can* and *do* sin, when we should improve, is just as wrong as any tendency to invent or live in fear of sins where they do not exist. It is difficult, of course, to keep one's equilibrium on the teeter-totter between scrupulosity and laxity, but keep it we must.

And if we do keep our equilibrium, our view of the individual Christian (oneself or another) is likely to be not only healthy but laced with a good dash of optimism. We will see, as did the early Christians, that the normal state (not just the ideal state, but the normal state in fact) of an individual Christian is that he is without serious sin, despite his various human and personal failings. At the same time, we would want not only to acknowledge the danger of seriously offending one's God and one's fellow man, but also to improve, as best we can, in the various areas where we can detect shortcomings.

It is in this light that the penitential liturgy of the

Church has undergone quite some development. As we observed previously in this chapter, the early penitential liturgy was generally reserved for those who had alienated themselves from the eucharistic community by a grievous sin, usually of a publicly scandalous nature; these were then pronounced as excommunicated, in a public ceremony, by the bishop as head of the eucharistic community, and were given a penance (usually long and arduous) to perform.[32] After completion of the prescribed penance, the penitent was welcomed back into communion with his fellow Christians in a joyous liturgy of reconciliation, normally culminating in celebration of the eucharist.[33]

Between the sixth and twelfth centuries, some evolution began to make its mark on the penitential liturgy. Public penitential ceremonies began to give way to private confession and subsequent absolution, and confession of venial sins began to be seen as a worthwhile practice for one's self-improvement and for a sharing in the graces of the sacrament of reconciliation.[34] The monastic practice in religious orders, as it has been passed down to our own century, has called for regular confession of sins—even though this would involve confessing only minor sins or repeating past failings—and this practice has been expected not only of clerics and religious-order members, officially, but also, unofficially, of the laity as a whole.[35] So it was that anyone who went through Catholic schools as recently as the 1960s can remember that confession was expected at least once a month, and more likely once a week.

It has recently become a current opinion that we would do well to not participate in confession so frequently as we have been led to in the past. A number of Catholics who take this opinion seriously now confess their sins only annually, in accord with the ecclesiastical precept,[36] and many do not do even that. As one person recently said to me: "I know that in my situation in life, there isn't much chance for me to get into serious trouble, morally, and I surely don't go *looking* for trouble. I'm not claiming that I have no imperfections, but I just don't see myself offending God or man in any serious ways! So why should I go to confession every week, or month, or even every year?"

Immediately, many would be wont to respond: "Because of the graces of the sacrament, you should go to confession as frequently as you can, even when you feel you have nothing to confess!" There is, perhaps, some truth to be gleaned from both points of view.

First of all, we should note that *grace* is a *relationship*, not a *substance*. Why make a point of that? Because for many of us, in our early years of religious education, grace was presented to us as a substance, as some kind of *stuff* or tangible matter (as a child, I usually thought of grace as resembling tapioca pudding): it came in buckets or milk bottles or some other kind of container, and you "got" some of it, and you could "spill" or lose it, or get a few extra "drops," or go back to the "grace-refilling" station, *et cetera ad nauseam*. If grace is truly *stuff*, then each of us should strive to have a cup that runneth over.

But grace is not stuff. The word *grace* comes from the Latin *gratia*, which is related to such English words as *gratuitous* (freely given or given when it needn't be). Further back, it is *charis* in the New Testament Greek, as derived from Hebrew roots *(hen* and *hesed)* wherein the Jews, in their existential vocabulary, described God's way of relating to man as being like that of a king who broke "protocol" by welcoming a lowly servant into his personal friendship.[37] Why all the linguistics? To point out that it is precisely the kind of *relationship* described in the Hebrew and Greek, even the more recent Latin, that is meant by our word *grace*. However, a funny thing happened to some of our theological Latin. Anyone who has ever taken Latin (especially out of the old Bennett *Latin Grammar*[38]) will remember that the Latin *res* could be translated into English as "thing, or anything else suited to the meaning of the sentence."[39] And so it was, when we had to translate passages from English to Latin, whenever we couldn't think of a Latin equivalent for a particular English noun, we tended to supply *res* in the appropriate case. Those who have studied the accommodated use of *res* in sacramental theology will understand it as "reality," i.e., the reality of grace of the sacrament and its sign *(res et sacramentum)*[40] or the reality of the sacramental grace in itself *(res tantum)*.[41] Unfortunately, the accommodated theological use of *res* seems to have become obscured, so that rather than refer to the relationship of individuals to God in grace as a living personal reality, we have tended to concretize the *res* of grace as a kind of "thing," or *stuff*, and thus a kind of stuff which can be measured quantitatively, be spilled, refilled, and so on. In light of this type of caricature, one can easily understand the argument that favors participation in each of the sacraments as frequently as possible, regardless of the meaning or purpose of the sacramental rite in question.

But if we think of grace as *living relationship*, in which a person grows as friend-of-God, then we cultivate some sympathy for the view that does not automatically require great frequency in the sacrament of penance and reconciliation. Rather, we tend to think of the individual Christian as growing in his relationship with God and man in a spirit that is genuinely penitential in its openness to the formative Word of God, and that genuinely seeks improvement of self as witness to Christ and his message in moral life, but which does not always require frequent participation in the penitential sacramental ritual as such.

But this does not mean that we should ignore the sacrament altogether. We will have recourse to it often enough, I think, when we realize our own inadequacy in our efforts to fulfill[42] ourselves as Christians, and also the important relationship of penance to eucharist as it has become manifest in the worship-life of the Church.

As we have said, the commission by a Christian, knowingly and willfully, of an act which had been revealed to him as seriously contradictory to the Gospel message, once he had been "dead to sin" in baptism,[43] was seen as something akin to treason. The grievous sinner was considered to have excommunicated himself from the community of the one Bread and the one Body in the eucharist. And it was expected that his readmission to this community involve at least as much thought and will as did the action which effected his leaving it. Thus the lengthy and rigorous penitential procedure, which by now has been relaxed substantially.[44] But when the re-entry was to take place, the re-entry was precisely in the context of the banquet of charity in the community of Christ, the eucharist.

This is in light of the realization that sin and grace, alienation and reconciliation, are basically not individual, but *communal* realities. We have noted before[45] that we celebrate our redemption in Christ's Passover in the New Covenant as a *community*, just as the Jews celebrate as a *community* their liberation in the Exodus/Covenant. So, too, do we emulate our Jewish forebears in ritualizing sin and forgiveness as communal realities: the Jews realized that one who sinned in the community took the whole community (however slightly) away from God, and that the whole community was responsible for the sins of all its individual members, and thus together asked forgiveness.[46] St. Paul, again utilizing the image of the Church as bodily organism, recognizes the same factor: one who cuts himself off from God by sin weakens the whole body, just as a diseased member of a physical body weakens the other members.[47] Another way of saying this could be that spiritual and moral health, or disease, can be contagious.[48]

So it is the *community* that is penitent when one or more among its members effects a weakening in the bonds of love between man and man, man and God, and it is the *community* that celebrates the making-well of the relationship once more in reconciliation.

This is why penance is celebrated communally in the Catholic tradition. It is true that we no longer speak of "excommunication" (although our penitential absolution prayers have contained a vestigial reference to it)[49] and that an excommunication or reconciliation ceremony conducted by the bishop is no longer a part of our liturgical experience. Penance now tends to be a private affair, and its sacramental ritual is officiated at normally by a priest as delegate of the bishop. But even here, we should realize the communal significance of our actions against man and God, and of our growth in grace by way of forgiveness and reconciliation.

In an attempt to highlight these meanings of the penitential sacrament, many Catholic communities have had recourse, of late, to "group celebrations" of penance, either regularly or occasionally. In some of the situations I have been familiar with, there is a brief service of the word, wherein readings, and perhaps a brief homily, will give the congregation an orientation to the meanings of sin and reconciliation, specifically in terms of their communal dimensions. Then an opportunity will be provided for the actual sacrament of reconciliation itself: sometimes by way of individual confession and counselling; sometimes with confession only, but no lengthy conversation between penitent and confessor; sometimes in the form of the members of the community turning to one another and asking for-

giveness for their sins, either in general, or with reference
to specific instances (presumably things already evident to
the community as a whole, and not personally secret). Often,
if confession takes some time, there is the chanting of psalms
or other prayers appropriate to the situation, in which the
individual members of the community join for their penitential prayers (this would often suffice for the "penance"
to be said). When all have confessed (or all that are going
to; those who do not wish to are not required to) absolution is often given (unless it has been given in confession
individually) and the service terminates in some sort of
celebration of joy in reconciliation—sometimes, most appropriately, in the eucharist itself.

Obviously, there are many variations on this theme, but
the basic pattern is an attempt to realize in a concrete way
the reality of the communal dimensions of sin, alienation and
reconciliation. And the experience is usually a good deal
more meaningful and attractive for today's Catholics than
would be their former experiences of "going to confession"
in days gone by.

However, some questions remain to be asked: to begin
with, should general absolution be given in such a situation,
without individual confession? It is clear from the most
conservative sources of Church authority that general absolution is valid and licit in certain special situations of a
grave nature,[50] so it follows that the Church may allow an
extension of the circumstances wherein general absolution
can be employed. But although that may be done, the question is, *should* it be done? My own reaction is in the negative. I say this not because I am hopelessly mired in any
archaic rigorisms or antiquated legalisms, but because I believe individual confession and absolution serve many important purposes, even though it is certain that these procedures may be foregone for grave reason.[51]

One of the important factors here, of course, has to do with the whole experience of being related to as an individual person, not just as a member of a larger aggregate . . . an individual with specific problems and orientations requiring individual attention. Another factor, closely related, is the need to in some way isolate and speak to some specific failings on one's own part, so that areas for necessary improvement can be spelled out. To simply say "I'm sorry for all the ways in which I have failed to love and be open towards others," or simply "I'm sorry" (as in the case of one penitential liturgy I heard of) may be very sincere. But it also strikes me as awfully vapid, and it could, especially if repeated with any frequency, become more meaninglessly mechanical than any of the old rituals we are so quick to criticize. Furthermore, it seems to fall short of the need for each individual to come to terms with himself as a Christian, to assess with some semblance of objectivity his own strengths and weaknesses, as they are manifest in attitudes and actions (thus the importance of a confessor who is a fair spiritual and moral guide).

Here it becomes necessary to effect a sort of balance: to adhere to the penitential-liturgy experience as it has been known in our past is to perpetuate a situation which (though often helpful for some, and thus not to be wholly abandoned) is often too frequent, too hurried, too high-pressure, too traumatic and too exasperating for many a Catholic, especially many a younger Catholic. Yet a taking-stock of one's development as a Christian requires a sort of healthy discipline not to be found in absenting oneself entirely from a structured penitential situation. To effect, at least for oneself if not also for numerous others, a penitential situation wherein confessor and penitent(s) may come together in ways which will be genuinely helpful and meaningful will require a good deal of effort (choice of confessor, of liturgical formats to be considered, etc.) but it should be well worth it. To do otherwise would be to give up too easily, and giving up too easily is precisely what Christianity is *not* all about.

1. Romans 6:10.

2. **Loc. cit.**

3. On WSOU in South Orange, New Jersey, from 1967-69; the broadcast in question was in March, 1968.

4. The chaplain was Rev. Henry J. Schreitmueller of Seton Hall University; the undergraduates were William Shlala of Seton Hall and Saralyn Hogan of St. Thomas Aquinas College, Sparkill, N. Y.

5. Romans 6:10.

6. **Loc. cit.**

7. Cf. Charles E. Curran, "Penance," in **Contemporary Problems in Moral Theology** (Notre Dame: Fides, 1970), Chapter 1.

8. **Ibid.**

9. This conversation took place in 1963.

10. Cf. Walter M. Abbott, ed., **The Documents of Vatican II,** q.v., pp. 675ff.

11. Cf. Joseph Fletcher, "Love Is the Only Measure," in **Commonweal** LXXXIII:14 (January 14, 1966), p. 427.

12. **Ibid.,** p. 428.

13. **Ibid.,** p. 431.

14. **Ibid.,** p. 427.

15. **Ibid.,** p. 429.

16. Herbert McCabe, "The Validity of Absolutes," in **Commonweal,** ibid., pp. 432ff.

17. **Art. cit.,** pp. 433ff.; I am paraphrasing McCabe's question here.

18. This is the way in which Charles Curran speaks of "natural-law absolutes." In a lecture given at the Spring, 1967, regional meeting of the College Theology Society at St. John's University in New York, Curran pointed out that the moral "absolutes" in Scholastic treatments of natural moral law generally are qualified by the phrase **ut in pluribus** (in most cases).

19. One may note here Kant's notion of the "categorical imperative" as ethical norm. Cf. Immanuel Kant, **The Critique of Pure Reason,** tr. N. K. Smith (London: MacMillan Co., Ltd., 1929).

20. Matthew 5:3-11; Luke 6:20-23.

21. Cf. Luke 2:25. The Jerusalem Bible translation differs slightly from the more familiar English words I have used.

22. Cf. Galatians 1:11-24.

23. I Corinthians 7:26.

24. **Loc. cit.**

25. I Corinthians 7:12.

26. Exodus 20:15.

27. Exodus 20:8-11.

28. Cf. Walter M. Abbott, ed., **op. cit.**, pp. 675ff.

29. James M. Megivern has made frequent use of this expression.

30. **E.g.,** H. Noldin & A. Schmitt, Comp., **Summa Theologiae Moralis** (Oeniponte: Typis et Sumptibus Feliciani Rauck, 1952).

31. Again I recall the insights of Eugene Kennedy. Cf. Chapter 2, **supra.**

32. Cf. Josef A. Jungmann, **The Early Liturgy to the Time of Gregory the Great** (Notre Dame, Ind.: University of Notre Dame Press, 1959), pp. 249ff.

33. Jungmann, **loc. cit.**, and **Public Worship: A Survey** (Collegeville, Minn.; The Liturgical Press, 1957), pp. 77ff.

34. Suso Mayer, "Devotional Confession," **Orate, Fratres XVIII** (1944), pp. 159ff.

35. **Ibid.**

36. **CIC,** Can. 906. (This canon actually refers to grave sin.)

37. John L. McKenzie, **Dictionary of the Bible** (Milwaukee: Bruce, 1965), pp. 324ff.

38. Charles E. Bennett, **Latin Grammar** (Boston: Allyn & Bacon, 1908), revised edition.

39. **Ibid.,** p. 29.

40. Cf. Gerald Pire, "The **Res et Sacramentum** in Four Contemporary Theologians" (Milwaukee, Wis.: Unpublished thesis, Marquette University, 1968).

41. **Ibid.**

42. I studiously avoid the word "perfect" here, for reasons to be explained in Chapter 8, **infra.**

43. Romans 6:10.

44. Cf. A. M. Henry and M. Mellet, "Penance," in A. M. Henry, ed., **Christ in His Sacraments (Theology Library VI)** (Chicago: Fides, 1958), p. 206.

45. In this chapter, **supra.**

46. Johs. Pedersen, **Israel** (Copenhagen: Dyva and Jeppesen, 1940), pp. 359-364.

47. Cf. I Corinthians 12:4-31; Ephesians 4:1-5:20.

48. The notion of health as "contagious" is not as terribly strange as it might sound. I can recall Prof. Nick J. Topetzes of the psychology faculty at Marquette frequently emphasizing the notion that "mental health, like

mental illness, is contagious" and can thrive, or not, in certain atmospheres or environments.

49. ". . . I absolve you from every bond of excommunication and interdict . . ." Cf. Philip T. Weller, tr., **The Roman Ritual** (Milwaukee: Bruce Publishing Co., 1950), Tit. III, Cap. 2.

50. **CIC,** Can. 901.

51. **Loc. cit.**

⟶⟪7⟫⟵

To Love In Christ

The Victorian era which preceded our present epoch was said to be an age of puritanism so far as sex was concerned. In reality, social critics now opine, it was an age in which sex was somewhat like the opposite of the weather; whatever people *did* about it, they didn't want to *talk* about it. Today, it is quite the contrary: whatever people do (or don't do) about sex, they feel a *compulsion* to talk about it. One of the weekly newsmagazines recently featured on its cover a display of the many "sex" books now making their impact on the respectable publishing market, with the headline "More Than You Ever Wanted to Know About Sex."[1] Perhaps the magazine's editors hit the nail on the head: today's society is so saturated with emphasis on sex that it tends not to be shocking, but simply to be boring.

How, we might ask, could sex ever become boring? Surely, it would seem, a sufficient number of qualified psychologists have determined the sexual character of so many of our unconscious and subconscious motivations. The basic role of sexuality in human life and experience seems undeniable. True enough. But we have managed to approach the saturation point so far as the discussion and display of sexuality is concerned, so that matters sexual tend to become routine in the public eye.

To a certain extent, this is doubtless a sign of some health. It is no longer presumed, for instance, that "nice" people should know nothing of reproductive anatomy and physiology, nor is it the convention to avoid any reference, in polite society, to anything which is even vaguely suggestive of sexuality: in the Victorian era, we are told, the "legs" of chairs and tables had to be referred to as "limbs" by people of good taste, and even within the past twenty years, the pregnant condition of Lucille Ball on the *I Love Lucy* TV series was considered such a delicate matter that, while the expectant Lucy was allowed to be televised and her condition written into the story, the word "pregnant" was banned from the air by the CBS continuity acceptance (censorship) department, even though clergymen representing various faiths had indicated to the network that there was nothing objectionable about the term.

However, we have been witnessing a swing of the pendulum to another extreme of late, so that many people have felt it necessary to proclaim their sexuality in ways which are excessive and tasteless, and which would be comic if they were not so tragic.

When I was a graduate student at Marquette, I found myself rooming with and near a number of freshmen from a variety of small Midwestern communities, who enjoyed frequenting our rooming house since they could drink beer there but not in the dormitories on campus. I was on the periphery of one of their Friday night sessions when the talk turned to sexual exploits. Each of the eighteen-year-olds, in turn, delivered himself of a tale which bested the adventurous narratives of the ones given previously. I made no comment, but was interested to notice that, within a week, each one of the undergraduates in the group came to me individually to admit: "Gee, George, I never did any of those things at all, but I had to say *some*thing for all the other guys!" This, I believe, is the stuff of which much of our current "sexual revolution" is made.

But I am not so naive as to suggest that there is no "sexual revolution" at all. To be sure, there is a revolution, a turning-around, in sexual attitudes which is clearly contrary to the Victorian spirit. Even if it can be argued (as it often enough is) that sexual *activity* is not terribly different today, sexual *attitudes* obviously are: sexual innocence, a prized distinction in decades past, is so looked upon with scorn today that an impressive amount of sexual experience must often be pretended, if not achieved.

Even this can be seen as a sign of health in some ways, just as a fever indicates that the organism is mustering the strength necessary to fight an infection. To a large extent, it is a part of our growing-up sexually as a society, our coming to a genuine realization that sexuality is not only an integral part of our humanity, but of our encounter with the divine, with our sacramental identity in and with Christ. Accordingly, we are coming to know that a certain emphasis, a certain celebration in fact, of our sexuality is in many ways an act of worship, a sacrament of our believing in the saving Incarnation. Thus it is healthy not only that we come to understand and proclaim what it means to be a sexed person, male or female, but also that we progress to more mature understandings of manliness or womanliness. (Today, for instance, we are coming to realize that a man does not become less masculine if he helps with the housework, or a woman less feminine if she pursues a profession.)

But just as a competent doctor would become concerned if his patient's fever began to go too high, or remain for too long a time, so ought we be somewhat concerned about some excesses in our "sexual revolution" today.

The great novelist Graham Greene has been quoted as saying that "sex is neither solemn nor dull."[2] If, in the past, we have committed the error of attaching to matters sexual an inordinate false solemnity, then today we run the risk of dulling our ability to appreciate human sexuality fully and with meaning.

Perhaps the chief symptom of this is the tendency we now have to seek a *quantity* of sexual experience or display at the expense of the *quality* of sexual affirmation and development. My wife, who has taught on the elementary and middle-school levels for years, tells the story of the psychiatrist who addressed a conference for teachers on the subject of sex education. In one school, the doctor said, he addressed a group of adolescent boys and asked them the question (which obviously had to be translated for some), "How many of you have experienced penile-vaginal penetration?" A large, perhaps surprisingly large, number of hands went up. Then the doctor asked the boys, "How many of you have experienced sexual intercourse?" For those who were quick to raise their hands again, the doctor pointed out that the second question referred to something *not* quite the same as the subject of the first, that there existed a profound difference, or a number of profound differences, between mating, or sexual experimentation, and expressing love.

Perhaps it was the spirit of the Victorian age that sexual activity was to be avoided when possible: that "nice" married couples engaged in coitus only to procreate, and that married couples beyond childbearing age were to avoid intercourse since they were "too old for that sort of thing." But today, it seems, we are at the other extreme: a male who has not had at least one sexual liaison by the age of eighteen will often find himself compelled to pretend that he has, and a female whose virginity has not been challenged by the age of twenty will often wonder whether or not she is sufficiently attractive as a woman.

And it is precisely in this sort of atmosphere that the

quality of sexual experience and sexual symbols stands in serious danger of being devaluated. The Victorians knew so little about sex, we would say. Perhaps they knew not its full meanings as sacrament, its real holiness, its true joy, its wonderful possibilities for genuine personal growth and understanding, its tremendous beauty. But they knew, even in a somewhat negative way, that it was *special.* That sexual communion somehow belonged with a very special sort of personal communion (whether or not the Victorians always acted according to the principle). I wonder if we know that today.

While I had some fine undergraduate courses in theology, one of the college courses in which I derived much religious insight was one in sociology, where the Jesuit professor[3] once discussed sex in these terms: Think, he said, of man's physical existence as you would think of a stained glass window. The window is *translucent,* in that you see the window in and for itself, but you also see light which shines through it. The solid wall is opaque: it shows only itself for itself, and permits no light to shine through. The clear window is transparent: it permits not only light, but other objects to be seen, while the window itself (especially if really clean) is practically unseen. If one thinks of man's physical existence, particularly his sexual nature, as an opaque wall, as in the hedonist view, he sees it only in and for itself, without the light of meaning or of the divine shining through. If he thinks of it as transparent, he will find it continually being justified or excused by external reasons but not valued for itself (as in the Puritan or Jansenistic view). We must reject both these extremes and allow ourselves to see human sexuality in and for itself, but also in its possibilities for meaning in relationships between man and woman, man and fellowman, man and God.

If we fail to appreciate the meanings of sexuality today,

I submit, it is perhaps because the approach of *translucence,* mentioned here, has been stifled by our being buffeted between the extremes of *opacity* and *transparence,* between the poles of hedonism on one extreme and Puritanism-Jansenism on the other. It is often said today that our young people are immoral when it comes to sex. I am by no means undistressed by the course which sexual activities and attitudes are taking at present, but I really wonder: is the problem one of people's having rejected morality (thus being truly *im*-moral) or is it because they have not been given a concept of morality, at least sexually, which is balanced and consistent within itself (in which case, probably, they might be *a*-moral)?

In one way, it can be said that Catholic moral teaching has concentrated too much on sex; in another, it can be argued that Catholic moral teaching has not said enough about sex, not spoken frankly and thoroughly enough to some of the issues involved. Let me give you an idea of what I mean here:

Suppose I were to admit that, late last Friday night, a young woman and I went together to the Holiday Inn motel in Omaha, Nebraska, and committed an immoral act. Many Catholics would assume that we had engaged in some sort of illicit sexual congress. It is entirely possible that we did no such thing, but instead robbed the motel manager's safe, or attended a racist rally in one of the motel's meeting rooms, or overindulged in alcohol in the motel bar. Any one of these, among other possibilities, could have been the "immoral act" in question. But for most people, especially most Catholics, an "immoral act" is almost always thought of as a *sexually* immoral act. In that way, Catholics are indeed an ecclesial body preoccupied with sex.

But for all of our preoccupation, real and exaggerated, with sex, we seem to understand—to even try to under-

stand—so little about human sexuality. When sexual topics
have come up for honest and open discussion, how often have
well-intentioned people stifled the discussion or "changed
the subject," thus providing ammunition for those who
would advocate sexual experimentation in the extreme as a
means of rebelling against the "hang-ups" of "straight"
society?

In our present milieu, we will doubtless observe myriad
attitudes or acts which betray sexual immaturity. These will
range from licentiousness to prudery. We do well to identify
and correct these when we can. We will do better to find
ways in which to envision and rectify the sexual immaturi-
ties that debilitate us as a *people,* specially as a Christian
people.

At the outset, it will be necessary to further clarify the
relationships between identity and sexuality. We are already
making some strides in this regard, in connection with some
of the pressures of our complex and changing society. It is
now the case, often, that wives will work while husbands
will baby-sit, that women will achieve positions in several
professions once thought to be the domain of "a man's
world," that men will become increasingly comfortable in
manifesting signs of tenderness, sensitivity and creativity
that once would have been branded "effeminate." We are
now coming to realize that a female can be none the less
feminine for being a personnel manager, and that a male
can be none the less masculine for cooking dinner after he
has picked up a few pointers from "The Galloping Gourmet"
on TV.

Some of the arguments of the current "women's liberation" movement have offended me and others because what
they would seem to advocate is female supremacy rather
than equality, or the preservation of privilege without responsibility. But true "women's liberation" must necessarily

be the liberation of men *and* women alike, a realization of the genuine equality in dignity and worth (although not identity or interchangeability) between the human sexes.

A few years ago, I was giving a lecture series on "Contemporary Moral Problems" to students at Rutgers University,[4] and was asked, "Do you believe in the double standard?" I immediately replied in the negative, but to make myself clear, it was necessary to point out that advocating "equality of sexual freedom" meant that men and women were both equally free to conduct their sexual activities morally, maturely and responsibly, and not that women were to be granted the same sort of license that is so often characterized by the *Playboy* image of the male.

To realize this will mean the destruction of some of our oldest sexual-moral myths, specifically as they are often grouped under the heading of "the double standard." It will mean to acknowledge that a woman is not a plaything for man, or a piece of property to be bought or sold, stolen or retrieved, who has no interior feeling or motivation. It will thus be acknowledged that women are just as responsible —no more and no less—for their moral actions as are men. A case in point (which might be disturbing to some of the more extreme women's libbers) would be adultery. Our mores have frequently suggested that the cuckolded husband is justified in his wrath as directed at "the other man," but that the wife, as unthinking piece of property, needs simply to be retrieved after the theft. Women will surely be held more responsible, more accountable, for their own part in this sort of situation if true "women's liberation" or "sexual equality" comes to fruition. *A fortiori,* we might wonder how often such a thing as "seduction" takes place, and to what extent the image of the female "victim" is accurate, if members of both sexes are equally in control of themselves and responsible for their actions.

Our arrival at a realization of genuine sexual equality
will be painful, perhaps gradual, and probably fraught with
occasional upheavals and setbacks. One factor involved here
will be the question of whether or not a discriminatory decision or practice is in reality sexually based (or, as they
say, sexist). Just as an illiterate may be refused a teaching
position on the grounds of illiteracy, without any aura of
racial discrimination entering the picture, so an unqualified
person may be denied an opportunity on the grounds of
lack of qualifications, and not on the basis of sex. Yet in
these times, it is frequently the case that the group which
has tended to suffer from discrimination will be quick to
recognize it whenever it exists, and even some times when
it doesn't. Thus those who have suffered the most racial
discrimination are quick to charge "racism," and those who
have suffered from sexual inequality will be quick to hurl
the epithet "male chauvinist pigs." The charge may not always be accurate, but it will often be made, and it will be
necessary to exercise as much patience as fairness in making
our way through the troubled waters.

Part of our problem concerning sexual identity has to do
with myths surrounding the roles of the sexes in procreation.
For centuries, it was believed that prenatal life in its entirety was contained in the male's semen, and that the female's uterus was but a receptacle for the development of
the semen into a person. The existence of such organs as
ovaries, which make their substantive contribution to the
formation of new life, was unknown. We now realize, medically, that the role of the mother in procreation is at least
as substantive as, and surely more complex than, that of
the father. This realization has helped us to develop a more
mature image of woman. But the myths that held on for
so long, until dispelled by scientific discovery, certainly
made their mark. One reason that they did was because of

the attention given the relationship between sexuality and procreation, and this is an area which surely must be explored if we are to understand sex and some of the moral options in our sexual lives.

Until recently, most Christians had been led to believe that sex was good, or barely tolerable, only in so far as it did, or could, lead to procreation. No serious theologian would want to assert that this was really the consistent and official teaching of the Church. It was but a distortion of Church teaching, and many of those who today rail against "Catholic teaching on sex" waste much ammunition fighting a caricature and not a reality.[5] But, be that as it may, that very sort of caricature has enjoyed great currency for a long time within the "folk-Catholicism" milieu, and has profoundly influenced the thoughts, words and deeds of generations of Catholics and others alike.

This has led to at least these two misconceptions: first, that the only justification for sexual activity is the possibility of progeny and, second, that the only form which sexual activity or self-assertion can take is ultimately genital, or venereal.

To swing at the second icon first: even in this age of debate over sexual identity, equality between the sexes, and so on, we surely realize that there is far more to masculinity, or to femininity, than possession of male or female physical characteristics and biological functions. Even to begin exploring or hinting at the depths of what it means, psychologically or emotionally, to be sexed as a male or female person, is to in some way incarnate this type of understanding. We can thus appreciate the fact that someone can be profoundly masculine without conquering young maidens, or deeply feminine without luring men into her boudoir. Further, it is surely possible for someone to be a real man without being a father, or a real woman without being a mother. And indeed, it is possible for someone to be genuinely feminine or masculine without asserting one's sexuality in genital activity, as in the case of the person who chooses, consciously and with dedication, the exercise of masculinity or femininity in the witness of the celibate religious life (although this can only become really true when celibacy becomes a genuine choice for Christians, and not a prerequisite for other choices having no necessary connection with one's being celibate or not).[6]

As for the first icon, we must note that (contrary to the caricatures so often criticized by many) traditional Catholic teaching in its essentials has not considered the possibility of procreation a condition for the exercise of licit genital sexual activity. Even that most conservative of Catholic sources, The Code of Canon Law, renders the inability to consummate intercourse an impediment to a valid marriage, but the inability to procreate is not so considered.[7] More recently, explicit Papal and magisterial approval of coitus when procreation is presumed impossible (periodic abstinence or "rhythm")[8] paved the way for the decision by the Fathers of the Church in Vatican Council II to omit from their Constitution on the Church in in the Modern World, in its section on marriage and family life, any reference to procreation as "primary end of marriage."[9] The expression and fostering of marital love, in itself and for its own sake—not as any sort of means or "secondary end"—is both in theory and fact an operative principle in Catholic moral teaching today. It is this factor (both before and since the debate emanating from Pope Paul VI's 1968 encyclical *Humanae vitae*)[10] which has helped countless Catholic theologians and others to understand sexual encounter as worthy of cultivation in its own right, and not something to be tolerated for a "higher good" in procreation.

This influence combined with a number of others over

the past century or so: the impact of the French personalist movement, the demise of the "marriage of convenience" and the arranged marriage, de-emphasis on the dowry, etc., so that a marital relationship comes to be seen as an end in itself, not simply a means to advantageous business mergers, good breeding or social and political liaison. One of the manifestations of this is the tremendous growth in marriages across the traditional ethnic, social, and geographic barriers, and even religious lines. And it is becoming more the case that people marry when it is virtually impossible to see how either one is "getting anything out of the deal." This in itself does not guarantee a happy marriage, but would at least indicate that the motivation is more likely to be one of genuine personal devotion to each other.

To accept this view of sexual encounter is to accept opportunities for more freedom in pursuing one's emotional, psychological and total personal development in union with another. Of this we can all be glad. It is also to accept much greater responsibility for these facets of development, and to face the exigencies of interpersonal relationships with far greater maturity than would have been envisioned in ages past.

Catholics are beginning to see changes in viewpoints in marriage becoming evident in the celebration of the marriage liturgy today. Often, the congregation is spared the "traditional exhortation" which insults the new spouses by continually reminding them of their obligation to procreate (they will likely do so anyway, without help from the superfluous material in the Collectio Rituum).[11] Often, the father no longer "gives the bride away" since she is an adult person making a free choice, and not a piece of property being traded off (and, probably, the difference between the father and the groom, socially, politically, or whatever, is such that the bride's father would never hand his daughter over to him willingly!). The nuptial couple often participate in the choice of music for the celebration (today, this often means folk hymns instead of Aunt Gertrude's operatic arias at the Offertory), and usually have their friends act as lector, commentator, etc., in a congregationally-participated liturgy.[12]

All of this indicates a tremendous awareness on the part of the young bride and groom (something which their parents may puzzle at) of the markedly personal character of their relationship to one another. It is as Tom Jones and Harvey Schmidt proclaimed in their musical *I Do! I Do!*

> Marriage is a sacrament
> which is just a way to say
> that a very private thing is done
> in a very public way.[13]

But at the same time, it indicates the tremendous responsibilities they bear to themselves and to each other for keeping their love alive and growing, and for allowing that love to truly be a sacrament of the love between Christ and his Church in the world.[14]

It is precisely in this context that I become distressed at some of the sexual extremes that I observe today, particularly the extreme of permissivism (the other extreme is barely in evidence any more), in that these extremes militate so insidiously against the quality of sexual symbols in personal relationships.

We have just emerged, it seems, from an era when it was considered admirable for a young man to know nothing of matters erotic until his wedding night, perhaps with the aid of a little "man to man talk" with his father shortly beforehand, and for a young woman to approach her bridegroom in ignorance. Most of the crude jokes about newlyweds (commonly told at bachelor parties) have their basis in that sort of custom, and—since many a truth is spoken in jest—point out the awful awkwardness, the gross misinformation, the damage to persons which could occur under such sorry circumstances. If that was the sort of era which preceded our own (and the reports, like those of Mark Twain's death, are no doubt greatly exaggerated) then we are well rid of it, and hopefully for good.

But I cannot see how the errors of the past would justify some of the widespread sexual experimentation that seems to prevail among even the youngest of adolescents, or the casualness with which many people exchange the deepest of sexual intimacies.

It might appear, at this juncture, that I am about to tell today's young people what they should or should not do. Not quite. I have been a teacher of college undergraduates long enough to know that, if I look like I am telling them how to conduct their lives, they will often enough (or too often) reject my words (or those of other teachers) in favor of their own experiences and insights. But I do feel that I can offer some thoughts on where those experiences and insights may lead, and on what decisions young people will, in the long run, be making for themselves.

It has been suggested that the sexual permissiveness of the present age might lead to another age of puritanical repression in sexual actions and attitudes. Those who hold this position maintain that the pendulum must swing again to the other pole, and they are quick to offer gory examples of contemporary depravity, sometimes exaggerated, but usually real enough: the Catholic grade school on Long Island where sixth-graders were regaled by a nun playing the song "Sodomy" from the original-cast album of *Hair;* the sex-education courses where students were encouraged to learn about anatomy by feeling strategic parts of each other's bodies; the religion classes where masturbation is commonly condoned, if not encouraged; the priest in New Jersey who told a group of college students that he couldn't really see that much wrong with premarital intercourse; and so on, *ad nauseam*.[15] And those who are appalled by such reports submit that we are entering a new age when sexual puritanism and repression will be the prevalent tone. They are not wrong in their anger over excesses and abuses, but I think they are wrong in surmising that a return to the Victorian age would find many supporters today. I do think, though, that we will see an exodus from the extremes, not towards puritanism, but towards a much more healthy and balanced outlook on sexual morality.

One of the characteristics of young people today is that they want their relationships to *mean* something. If they have rebelled against some of the moral teachings of the past, perhaps it was because these dicta did not offer to them an adequate sense of personal meaning. If premarital intercourse was proclaimed to be wrong, it was because of the threat of unwanted pregnancy or venereal disease; if masturbation was identified as wrong, it was because it could cause insanity or pimples. And so on. Now we know enough medically, and have the ability, to dismiss such threats. But so many of our sexual teachings in even the recent past were so rife with these threats that, when the threats evaporated, there was often nothing to take their place. The logical conclusion, for many young people, has been to assume that "the lid is off" and "anything goes." But, as I noted before, their own experiences and insights will soon indicate otherwise.

Today's young generation insists on experiences full of symbols and meanings. They may not be the symbols which sufficed for previous generations, but they will be symbols nonetheless. To be valid symbols, our young people will demand, they must have meaning. And in the age of sexual permissiveness, our young people seem ripe for a revolution against the widespread use of sexual symbols without meaning.

It is the older generation, especially clergymen, teachers and parents, who are castigated so often today as the heralds of a rather strict or "careful" sexual morality; tomorrow, I believe, it will be young people themselves.

It will be the young people themselves, probably, who will come to insist on the cautious use of sexual symbols . . . not because they are puritans, but because they are determined to celebrate and proclaim their sexuality, but only in meaningful terms. It will be the young people, today criticized for their complicity in a counter-culture of dispensability and planned obsolescence, who will insist on the stability of marital relationships. It will be the young, so often scored for their alleged promiscuity, who will come to assert that sexual relationships can be truly satisfying and full of personal meaning only when the exchange of sexual intimacies is reserved for relationships which are permanent and exclusive. I am not saying that all of this will happen instantly, but I do see the trend developing. Today's collegians, especially, are just a bit too young to be rebelling against Victorianism, although they may remember vestiges of its influence. If they react against anything, it will likely be the crypto-permissiveness of "middle-class morality" which manifests itself in a thousand suburbs where the decent-literature committees and the wife-swapping parties are too often composed of the same people.

What I am saying here, then, is that today's young, in the long run at least, will appear outwardly less reserved—perhaps even less respectful—about sex, but that in their inward thoughts, as manifest in their ways of life, they will be far less ready to use sexual symbols casually and frivolously than we would suspect. And if, indeed, they manage to become a generation that will be chaste without being prudish, moral without being a-sexual, and—in the best senses of the word—"sexy" without being salacious, they will have achieved a great deal for themselves and for others as well.

1. **Newsweek,** August 24, 1970.

2. Cf. Graham Greene, **May We Borrow Your Husband?** (Harmondsworth, Middlesex, England: Penguin Books Ltd., 1969).

3. Rev. Eugene J. Schallert, S.J., now director of the Institute for Socio-Religious Research at the University of San Francisco.

4. In 1968, under the auspices of the Rutgers-Douglass Newman Association.

5. **Ibid.,** Many superficial treatments of Catholic faith and practice ignore such distinctions, e.g., Michael F. Valente, **Sex: The Radical View of a Catholic Theologian** (Milwaukee: Bruce, 1970).

6. One can only imagine how many religious have chosen careers as teachers, nurses, administrators, etc., without consciously choosing the requirement of celibacy that was attached to their vocational choices. In such instances, not only is the witness value of celibacy virtually non-existent, but the risk of the individual's abandoning either the celibate state or the active service of the Church is ever present.

7. **CIC,** Can. 1068.

8. Cf. Robert G. Hoyt, ed., **The Birth Control Debate** (Kansas City, Mo.: NCR Publications, 1969).

9. **Ibid.**

10. **Ibid.**

11. Walter J. Schmitz, ed., **Collectio Rituum Pro Dioscesibus Civitatum Foederatarum Americae Septentrionalis** (Milwaukee: Bruce, 1964), pp. 456f.

12. Cf. George Devine, "Marriage—A 'Social Sacrament,'" **Topic** magazine section, **The Advocate,** May 5, 1968. Also George Devine, "Suggestions for a Revised Catholic Marriage Liturgy" (Chicago: submitted **ad usum privatum** to the Committee on the Revision and Adaptation of Rites, Subcommittee of the Bishops' Commission on the Liturgy, October 7, 1967).

13. Tom Jones and Harvey Schmidt, **I Do! I Do!** Copyright © 1966 by Tom Jones and Harvey Schmidt. Used by permission of Chappell & Co., Inc.

14. Cf. Devine, **op. cit.,** and Ephesians 5:21-32.

15. All of these sorry examples can be mentioned by name and place but obviously have not been so as to spare unnecessary embarrassment.

—»•[8]•«—

We Are In the World

The world, to a child, is a marvelous place full of an ever-increasing number of pleasant and exciting discoveries: ice cream, Santa Claus, a trip to the zoo, lemonade, the circus. Even when we begin to emerge from childhood, the luster of the world remains. As the theme song from the old "Aldrich Family" series used to begin each program, "All the world's a wonderland when you're in your teens. . . ."[1] And when we become young adults, the glories of the world seem greater than its pitfalls, and we are sure that we can capitalize on the former while managing to avoid or triumph over the latter. It is only when we become a bit older or more experienced that we can agree with these words attributed to John F. Kennedy: ". . . sooner or later, the world is going to break your heart."[2]

We have just come through an age when the Church seems to have shifted gears somewhat in relation to the world, or the *saeculum* of time-and-place, here-and-now. It seems, previously, as though the Church wanted to avoid too much contact with the world, to steer clear of its hazards. But in light of the spirit that typified and was characterized by Vatican Council II, Christians have been urged to take more seriously the redemptive Incarnation of the Word of God, and the involvement of Christ and his members in

the world that he comes not to destroy, but to save. In this
context, we can see the world as a potential sacrament of
the unity of man and man, man and God.

In the first chapter of this book, we surveyed some of the
disappointments that came to many men, most of all Christians perhaps, during the "decade of disillusionment" just
past.[3] And we might wonder where we are to turn next. To
the re-establishment of a neo-monastic isolationism, or of
the old "Catholic ghetto" where we snuggled up close to
our co-religionists inside a fortress Church that cowered
from the challenges of the world around us? No. Like the
apostles, we must learn that the entry of the Holy Spirit
and his life-giving force is our cue to exit from the secure
seclusion of the upper room. But we also know, now, that
to rush headlong into every possibility the world has to offer,
with all the naïvete of Pollyanna, is surely not going to work.
When I say "not going to work," I am not saying that prag-
matism must be the cardinal rule for Christianity. *Au con-
traire,* Christianity's greatest strengths often reside in its
visionary unwillingness to limit its options to the purely
pragmatic. Yet we know that the Christian life is not made
any less Christian for being workable, and that a series of
failures can be severely debilitating to even those inspired
by the very Word of God. Many times, in the Gospels, Jesus
tells his followers that they are deluded if they expect to
succeed in terms of the world, but he never says that they
should strive to fail.

Today's college generation may come to be described as
one which expects very little from the world. My own age-
group (those now thirty or older) is probably the one that
came to expect far too much from it. Our religious instruction, particularly within the confines of parochial schools,
had many things right with and many things wrong with it.

One thing wrong with it, I now believe, was its tendency to prepare us most admirably for perfection, but not for disappointment or failure. My age group, it seems now, was the one that was allowed to grow up believing that not too many things would really go wrong, and then found that practically everything could, would or did. The shock would not have been nearly so great, I think, had we been given some idea of how to deal with failure.

We have often heard the expression, especially in athletics, that it takes more talent to be a good loser than to win. Many of our teachers, with the best of intentions, seem to have spent much time teaching us how to "win," how to perfect ourselves so as to be living members of a "City of God" where perfection was the order of the day even in the midst of the world. But, I fear, they did not really prepare us to lose, or to come to terms with our imperfections, disappointments and failures. We were so often told how good we were, or must become, whether in academics, in sports, in the practice of our religion, or whatever, that we were genuinely unprepared for the experience of not coming up to par. Against this background, the events of the sixties, which for most of us were the events of early adulthood, came as a more horrible shock than they might have been for others. In a most painful way, we learned a lesson that has probably already been learned, to some extent, by those who have come after us. To expect the world—or the Church in the persons of its many all-too-human members —to be perfect, or even very good all the time, is to invite disillusionment. One must be prepared to admit that things can go wrong, that people can be hurt or even do the hurting, that the Gospel of Jesus the Christ has not managed, even after nearly two thousand years, to eliminate from the Christian community, let alone the world-at-large, avarice, fear, dishonesty, jealousy, pride, hatred and all of the other things which we know are so contradictory to the person and message of the Lord.

Yet we can—but must not!—fall so easily into the trap of a resigned pessimism. To assume that Christ is no longer with his Church or its members severally is to despair, to throw in the towel, to fail to witness to the very real presence of God which is all around us. If we realize that life will hold for us disappointments which we never would have expected, we must also acknowledge that it also will hold for us a series of "mini-miracles," if you will, that are equally unexpected.[4] Recently *The Critic* published on its cover a question put to Leon-Josef Cardinal Suenens of Belgium, "Why are you a man of faith, even in these days?" and his reply:

> Because I believe that God is new every morning, I believe that God is creating the world today, at this very moment. He did not just create it in the long ago and then forget about it. That means that we have to expect the unexpected as the normal way God's Providence is at work.
>
> That "unexpected" of God is exactly what saves and liberates us from determinism and from the sociologism of gloomy statistics about the state of human affairs in the present. That "unexpected," since it comes from God, is something coming out of his love for us, for the betterment of his children.
>
> I am hopeful, not for human reasons or because I am optimistic by nature, but because I believe in the Holy Spirit present in his Church and in the world—even if people don't know his name. I am hopeful because I believe that the Holy Spirit is still the creating Spirit, and that he will give us every morning fresh freedom, joy

and a new provision of hope, if we open our soul to him.

The story of the Church is a long story, filled with the wonders of the Holy Spirit: we must remember the saints and the prophets bringing, in hopeless times, a gulfstream of graces and new lights to continue on the road.

I believe in the surprises of the Holy Spirit. The Council was such a surprise, and Pope John was another. They took us aback. Why should we think that God's imagination and love might be exhausted?

Hope is a duty, not just a nicety. Hope is not a dream, but a way of making dreams become reality.

Happy those who dream dreams and are ready to pay the price to make them become true![5]

To call Cardinal Suenens, who has suffered "the slings and arrows of outrageous fortune"[6] as much as any of us, a naïve child is to be both inaccurate and grossly insulting. Yet he maintains the type of playfulness, if you will, the kind of childlike awe of the power of God, that should typify all Christians who have witnessed Jesus' triumph over sin and death in his saving resurrection.

To say that the salvific grace of the Risen Lord abounds in the world is not the same thing as saying that it has indeed been absorbed by the world. We are all too aware of the fact that much of the world as we know it appears to remain resistant to the love and faith of the Christian Gospel, and that to continue to proclaim that Gospel is to invite hardships which we cannot foresee even at this vantage point. Yet we must be like Peter, the prototype of all Christians in their imperfect humanness, who said to Jesus: "Lord, who shall we go to? You have the message of eternal life, and we believe. . . ."[7]

To believe that message is to come to grips with the "human condition" in the world as we know it, to assess with a real shrewdness the possibilities for Christian witness in the here-and-now, to exercise with real dexterity our own potentialities for making the love and faith of Christ's body, the Church, more manifest where we find ourselves, and to give full play to what can be achieved, as well as to realize what has not yet been achieved. And it is to take seriously the prayer which John describes Jesus as uttering to the Father for us:

I am not asking you to remove them from the world,
but to protect them from the evil one . . .
Consecrate them in the truth;
your word is truth.
As you sent me into the world,
I have sent them into the world,
and for their sake I consecrate myself
so that they too may be consecrated in truth.
I pray not only for these,
but for those also
who through their words will believe in me.
May they all be one.
Father, may they be one in us,
as you are in me and I am in you,
so that the world may believe
it was you who sent me. . . .[8]

1. "The Aldrich Family" on radio usually played an instrumental theme, but these words were sung in the introduction to the TV series (both on NBC during the late 1940s and early 1950s).

2. The entire quotation is "You're not truly Irish until you realize that, sooner or later, the world is going to break your heart."

3. The phrase is taken from John Cogley. Cf. Chapter 1, **supra**.

4. Obviously, "miracle" in the technical sense is not implied here.

5. **The Critic**, November-December 1970. With permission.

6. William Shakespeare, **Hamlet III**, 1.

7. John 6:69.

8. John 17:15-22.